Wildflowers

of Northern California's Wine Country & North Coast Ranges

A photographic guide to native plants of
Marin, Sonoma, Napa & Mendocino Counties

Reny Parker

Photographs by the Author

New Creek Ranch press
Cloverdale, CA 95425

ISBN-13: 978-0-9790430-0-0
ISBN-10: 0-9790430-0-X

Printed in China
First Edition/Second Printing

CAUTION
Ingesting plants or plant parts poses a potentially extreme health hazard and could result in sickness or even death. No one should attempt to use any wild plant for food or medicine without adequate training by a fully qualified professional. The author, publisher, and all others associated with the production and distribution of this book assume no liability for the actions of the reader.

The Wild Flower's Song
As I wandered the forest,
The green leaves among,
I heard a Wild Flower
Singing a song.
William Blake

Dedication

This book is dedicated to the memory of my father, Mel Stricklett. My thanks to him for taking me into the wilderness of central Oregon and British Columbia as a child. I owe my love of the outdoors to him.

For my husband and partner on the path of life, Keith, much love and appreciation for his unwavering support and encouragement to fulfill my desire to share the beauty of wildflowers with others. He's traveled many a backroad, being patient enough to pull over every 100 feet when flowers were spotted. Thank you, Dear.

Jai Guru Dev

Acknowledgements

A guide to wildflowers is a project usually not completed without the help of many other plant loving people. That is certainly the case with this guide. As a photographer who's main goal is sharing the beauty of wildflowers with others, assistance of botanists and those more knowledgeable than I was a necessity. A team consisting of Marianne Perron, Sarah Gordon, Liz Parsons, M.L. Carle, and Jonathan Akre started working to get the basic descriptions needed for the 360 species, 83 plant families, native to our four counties, to be included in the guide.

Photos were taken throughout the counties and special permission was obtained for entry and use of the following preserves: The Bishop's Ranch with assistance from Sean Swift; Fairfield Osborn Preserve with assistance from Julia Clothier and Nathan Rank; Pepperwood Preserve with the assistance of Michael Gillogly. At Sea Ranch I was given the royal treatment by Elaine Mahaffey, *Wildflowers of The Sea Ranch*, who shared generously of her time and knowledge. We had several great outings when the wildflower devas were definitely with us. Dea Freid spent a day introducing me to the salt marshes of Doran Beach Park.

Help with confirming the identification of plants was an ongoing process which started with Phil Van Soelen and Liz Parsons. Added later in the process were Nancy Harrison, Lori Hubbart, Peter Warner, Doreen Smith, Peter Baye, Richard Whitkus, Betty Young, Betsy Livingstone, Roger Raiche, and Alison Colwell.

For those plants that I was unable to photograph myself, the following friends contributed their talents: Doreen Smith, Mary Killian, Vishnu, Daniel F. Murley, Peter Baye, Gerald and Buff Corsi, Bob Case, and Charles Younger.

Writing text from the initial information gathered for 360 plants was an onerous task taken on by Timlynn Babitsky and Daniel F. Murley. Many hours were spent making these entries an interesting read. Help with the proofing of these came from Coralee Dey, Liz Parsons, Nancy Harrison, Betsy Livingstone, and Sherry Battisti.

Plant family descriptions were written by Betsy Livingstone and Sherrie Althouse. Garden use information was provided by Peigi Duvall and Kevin Bryant.

Final review of plant identification and descriptions were performed by Liz Parsons, Phil Van Soelen, Betty Young, Richard Whitkus, Peter Baye, Nancy Harrison, and Betsy Livingstone. Doreen Smith was a tremendous help with the second printing.

Information on hot spots for wildflowering were contributed by Lori Hubbart and Vishnu, Mendocino County; Doreen Smith, Marin County; Margaret Barson, Napa County; and CNPS Milo Baker Chapter board members for Sonoma County.

Initial feedback on cover designs came from Mila Mintun, with later review from John Kremer. Title suggestions came from many, but William Hathaway was a great source. There was input and "voting" by friends to help decide which cover to use.

Kathy Biggs, *Common Dragonflies of California*, and Taylor Lockwood, *Treasures from the Kingdom of Fungi*, gave advice on publishing. John Malpas of Calflora was extremely helpful with tips to make the most of their online database.

Plant family icons were illustrated by Tenaya Gordon. A young woman with a talent for giving tiny icons character.

Book layout was performed by myself with amazing email/phone tutoring by Sue Knopf. A woman with a great deal of patience and skill in Adobe InDesign.

Two people were constant throughout the process of this project: Liz Parsons, a guiding light for those working with natives plants in Sonoma County; and my husband, Keith, continually giving his support for me to make this guide the best that it could be. The introduction is his handy work as well as the short poems accompanying some of the images, for which I thank him. His ability to spot wildflowers is unsurpassed.

To all of these fellow lovers of wildflowers who came forward to make the dream of this photographic guide a reality, I heartily thank you.

Throughout the photographing, editing, proofing, and publishing, the duties were on my shoulders. For all but the photography I was in Fairfield, Iowa. There I participated in the Transcendental Meditation Program for World Peace, and with that was able to keep most of my sanity.

For additional images and updates see RenysWildflowers.com/guide.html.

I hope that by sharing the beauty of wildflowers and my enthusiasm for them, others will be inspired to care for these delicate gifts of nature and preserve them and their habitats for future generations.

Contents

Mule Ears...
robust parties climb dry hills
and mountains to 7,000 ft
handsome home to
painted lady butterflies

Introduction

USING THIS GUIDE

Use this guide to identify wildflowers native to Marin, Sonoma, Napa, and Mendocino counties. For our purposes, wildflowers are native flowering plants that grow and die in one year, annuals. Woody stem perennials are also included, as are a representative number of ferns, grasses, vines, shrubs and trees, and five examples of invasive (alien) weeds.

In this guide, wildflowers are identified with close up color photographs accompanied by non technical descriptions. Photographs and text are directed toward the curious as well as serious enthusiasts. Wildflowers are arranged by color. Within each color section photographs are arranged by the number of petals on a flower. Species likely to be confused are placed near each other to facilitate comparison of features. The sections for Ferns & Grasses and Vines, Shrubs, Trees are arranged by category and then alphabetically by Latin family name. Eighty-three families are included in the guide. Icons are used to convey family features. Readily available sources offering details on other botanical information are referenced.

A Field Guide to Pacific States Wildflowers was used to classify a flower's color. Because colors can range across a spectrum, the flower may not be found in the expected color section. In this case, go to the next most likely color. For these difficult plants, let shape be your guide.

Entries include common name, genus and species, and plant family. The online *Treatment from the Jepson Manual* was used as the definitive source for botanical names. Bear in mind that botanical names are now in constant flux and some plants may have been moved to a different family. To the best of my ability, these changes are noted to reflect the current name. There are often synonyms for names, and occasionally one will be listed. Common names may vary according to region, and some plants have several to many different names and various spellings. I have presented the one name that seems to be used most frequently in our area. Family icons are shown to aid in identification. Also included are leaf shape, similar species, plant rarity, natural history, and use by Native Americans. Wildflowers appropriate for gardening are noted—being adapted to local conditions, natives are easier to grow, require less water, provide food and habitat for local fauna, and are in all ways better for the environment than exotic species. Plants should never be taken from the wild. Besides often being illegal, it is best to leave them for all to enjoy, and for their natural cycle to be completed. Sources for purchasing plants are listed under Resources. Sizes are usually indicated by a range. To aid in identification, bloom times and counties where the plant may be found are listed. The county abbreviations are equivalent to: Ma, Marin; So, Sonoma; Na, Napa; Me, Mendocino. All photographs are by the author except those few noted with a colored dot • under the image; credit is given in Photo & Illustration Credits.

Rare and endangered plants are noted. Seismically fractured uplifts, erosion and settling render unique soils and habitats which foster rare plants. Urbanization and agricultural development, livestock grazing…and invasion of weedy and non native plants endanger wildflowers confined to habitats with limited range. Species flowering in wetlands and vernal pools are particularly vulnerable.

The abundance and variety of wildflowers throughout the region results from its diverse landscape, climate, and plant associations. The remainder of this introduction serves as a brief guide to these environmental features—features that make wildflowering a unique, sometimes challenging, but always fulfilling experience in the wine country and North Coast Ranges. And finally, learn tips on the secrets of successful wildflowering.

LAND

The land bears marks of the way it was formed. The major feature of mountains, hills and valleys run north northwest, a direction wrenched from the oceanic Pacific Plate and the North American Plate sliding past each other.

On the western edge of Marin County, the Point Reyes

Peninsula has been riding on the Pacific Plate for more than 300 miles. Sandy, loose soils from multiple periods of upliftment and erosion predominate. Inland of Point Reyes, the line through the Bolinas Lagoon, Olema Valley and Tomales Bay traces the San Andreas Fault—and is a rough demarcation between Pacific and North American Plates.

The land east of the San Andreas fault—and where most photographs in this book were taken—sits on the North American Plate. This crinkled and beautiful topography results from three interacting forces: uplift, erosion and faulting. The squeeze play between the Pacific and North American Plates uplifts mountains and hills. Erosion smoothes and rounds the rising land. The mountainous and hilly soils of the Coast Range and Mayacamas are often flinty and thin. Serpentine and/or a Serpentine complex (Serpentinite) are common. Soils deposited in faults by rivers and changing sea level fill lowland valleys. Valley soils run deep and rich, and are composed of sand, silt and clay in varying amounts. Much of Mendocino County straddles major faults and tilts west to exposed headlands before dropping into the Pacific.

WEATHER

The Pacific Ocean spreads its weather from west to east across all four counties.

Fog: From April through September wind and fog are common along the coast from Marin to Mendocino. At night, cooling fog creeps eastward along Navarro and Russian Rivers, fogging Anderson and Alexander Valleys, and the lowlands of the Santa Rosa area until midday, when the fog is usually burned off by the summer sun. Fog in eastern Mendocino and Sonoma counties (Ukiah, Sonoma Valley and Valley of the Moon…) and further east in Napa Valley is far less common. In Marin the fog blows through the Golden Gate, and up and over Mt. Tamalpais spilling onto the western shore of San Francisco Bay.

Precipitation: The rainy season extends from October to April. Precipitation decreases from north to south, and from west to east. On a wet year the western slopes of the coast range can receive 100 inches, while in a dry year the eastern reaches of Napa County receive less than 20 inches. In a typical year, coastal bluffs average 45 inches of rain, while inland Napa Valley sees 25. The middle areas of Alexander Valley, Dry Creek and Santa Rosa receive intermediate amounts, averaging 40 inches. Marin County receives 35 to 40 inches, on average. More rain falls on mountaintops than in valleys. Snow falls on the higher peaks nearly every winter. Snow, however, rarely accumulates more than a few inches and lasts from only days to a week in a typical year.

Temperature: As with precipitation, the Pacific Ocean is the dominant influence on the range in temperature. Coastal areas are cool throughout the year, averaging 40^0 to 68^0 F. Along the coast, temperature poorly indicates seasons, and sometimes one has to think, "Is this December or July?" Marin, being farthest south and moderated by San Francisco Bay on its east side, is warmer with a broad range in temperatures from 40^0 to low 80s. The inland valleys have the greatest range in temperature, averaging 36^0 to 90^0. Periods of freezing temperatures in winter and hot $+95^0$ days in summer occur every year. Upland areas are cooler by as much as 5 to 10 degrees.

ASSOCIATIONS

Wildflowers associate with plants that affect lighting, soil composition, moisture and nutrients.

Proximity to water defines low lying habitat. Salt marshes arc around the northern reaches of San Francisco Bay and along the shores of Tomales and Bodega Bays. Dunes occur on the Point Reyes Peninsula and near the mouths of Tomales Bay and the Russian River. Freshwater marshes occur at lower elevations near rivers and creeks, and in shallow depressions that remain moister than surrounding environs throughout the year. Examples include Cunningham Marsh and Laguna de Santa Rosa, both notable for their unique vegetation. Vernal pools, characterized by long term inundation followed by desiccation, were at one time common on flat valley floors, but to a large extent have been eliminated by industrial, residential and agricultural development. Riparian habitats of willow, alder, Oregon Ash, Big Leaf Maple…follow rivers and streams through valleys and into the hills.

Along the western edge of Sonoma and Mendocino counties, grasslands cover bluffs overlooking the Pacific. Despite development, grasslands dominate inland valleys and hills. Chaparral is found on exposed slopes that are relatively dry with good drainage.

Forests of oak, buckeye and madrone ascend the inland hills and occur in species specific stands as well as in mixtures. Shrubs—Coyote Brush, Snowberry, Elderberry…—can accompany these hardwoods.

Conifers are found throughout, where species and abundance depend on proximity to the Pacific and elevation. Redwoods dominate coastal canyons—as well as deeper inland valleys of the North Coast Ranges. Douglas-fir dominate the western reaches of Marin, Sonoma and Mendocino counties, and are found at higher elevations receiving adequate rainfall, but are uncommon east of Napa Valley. Pines occur along the coastal strip and at higher elevations inland. Digger Pines prefer rocky soil and like it hot—and are one of the few tree species that increase in abundance from west to east.

ENJOY (The Secret)

There's pleasure in wildflowering. Drive leisurely along scenic backroads under spring and summer skies. At the splash of color along the road's margin, stop the car, get out, stretch and breathe in pure Pacific air. This guide in hand, leave your car behind and walk the fields, woods and trails…along the ocean's edge. Kneel down to get a closer look at this peak of color, an expression that has no equal, independently and completely beautiful in its own right. Self realized. Open this guide and introduce yourself to a natural beauty God created and man named.

Plant Family Descriptions & Icons

Adder's-tongue, *Ophioglossaceae*
This family is more primitive than other ferns and can be distinguished by the leaves opening laterally. The spore cases are sacks on the stalk or at the base, lacking the dots on the underside of the leaves common to ferns. Worldwide 4 genera, 70 species, 3 species native in our 4 counties. Example: Grape Fern.

Amaranth, *Amaranthaceae*
Mostly annual herbs, but rarely also shrubs or small trees, with small bisexual or unisexual flowers, often prickly. Leaves are usually simple, alternate. It includes the plants formerly treated as Goosefoot, *Chenopodiaceae,* family. Worldwide 65 genera, 900 species, 5 species native in our 4 counties. Example: Goosefoot.

Arum, *Araceae*
In California a perennial herb, terrestrial or aquatic. Usually with a short erect vertical stem and leaves being simple or compound and basal. Generally a spike of ill smelling flowers. Example: Yellow Skunk Cabbage.

Bald Cypress, *Taxodiaceae*
Evergreen trees, conifers, male and female flowers on the same tree (monoecious), soft linear leaves, simple, not in bundles or scaled. Small woody seed cone. Grows in groves to great height and great age along coastal ridges, fog belts in limited distribution. Worldwide 10 genera, 16 species, 1 species native in our 4 counties. Example: Coast Redwood.

Barberry, *Berberidaceae*
Herb or shrub, may be perennial, deciduous or evergreen. Leaves of shrubs may be holly like or have spiny stems. Flowers generally with 6 petals borne singly or in clusters. Worldwide 9-16 genera, 590-670 species, 2 genera native to North America, 11 species native in our 4 counties. Examples: Inside-out Flower, Vanilla Leaf.

Birch, *Betulaceae*
Tree or shrub with cone like catkins or nuts. Leaves are deciduous, alternate with pinnate veins, usually toothed. Worldwide 6 genera, 105 species, 4 species native in our 4 counties. Example: Alder.

Bluebell, *Campanulaceae*
Annual or perennial, sometimes shrub or tree. Single bell shaped flowers, usually blue. Most have simple, alternate leaves and usually milky sap. Worldwide 70 genera, 2,000 species, 12 genera in North America, 25 species native in our 4 counties. Examples: Downingia, Harebell.

Borage, *Boraginaceae*
Annual, perennial, or shrub, often covered with stiff hairs, some cause dermatitis. Small flowers of 5 sepals and 5 petals often found on coiled spikes. Flowers mature sequentially as the coil unwinds. Worldwide about 100 genera, 2,000 species, 22 genera native to North America, 79 species native in our 4 counties. Examples: Hound's Tongue, Popcorn Flower.

Bracken, *Dennstaedtiaceae*
Perennial from rhizome. Leaf stalk strongly grooved on upper side, with generally 1-5 or more pinnate blades. Worldwide about 17 genera, 375 species, 1 species native in our 4 counties. Example: Bracken fern.

Broom-rape, *Orobanchaceae*
Annuals and perennials without leaves or chlorophyll, parasitic on the roots of other plants. The tubular flowers with upper and lower lips are comprised of 5 united petals and contain 2 pairs of 2 stamens each. Worldwide 14 genera, 200 species, 4 genera native to North America, 15 species native in our 4 counties. Examples: Clustered and Naked Broomrape, California Groundcone, various Monkey Flowers have been moved to this family.

Buckeye, *Hippocastanaceae*
Trees with deciduous, opposite palmate leaves. Large, glossy brown nutlike seeds. Flowers in showy, erect panicles have 4 or 5 separate petals. Late summer dormancy. Worldwide 2 genera, 15 species, only 1 species native in North America and in our 4 counties. Example: California Buckeye.

Buckthorn, *Rhamnaceae*
Small trees or shrubs with visibly 3 part berries or capsules. Simple, alternate, or opposite leaves. Small blue, white or greenish flowers are mostly regular and typically form in showy clusters. There are 4-5 petals, sometimes the petals are absent. Worldwide 58 genera, 900 species, 10 genera in North America, 58 species native in our 4 counties. Example: Ceanothus.

Buckwheat, *Polygonaceae*
Mostly annuals or perennials, sometimes shrubs or vines, rarely trees. Flowers are small with parts usually in multiples of 3, colored sepals, and no petals. Flowers often in clusters or heads with swollen nodes on stems. Seeds are often triangular. Worldwide 30-50 genera, 1,000-1,100 species with some cultivated for food, 15 genera in North America, 85 species native in our 4 counties. Example: Buckwheat.

Buttercup, *Ranunculaceae*
Most are leafy annuals and perennials, some vines. Flowers are radial or bilateral; the floral parts are of an indefinite number and separately attached. Many have medicinal or toxic properties. Worldwide 35-70 genera, 1,700-2,000 species, 23 genera in North America, 67 species native in our 4 counties. Examples: Columbine, Clematis, Meadow Rue, Delphinium, and Buttercup.

Cacao, *Sterculiaceae*
Shrub, trees, or herbs, often covered with star shaped hairs. Flowers are sometimes showy, often with 3-5 petal like sepals fused at the base, sometimes no petals, or 5 small petals fused to filament tube, separate stamens united by filaments fused below into a tube. Worldwide 50-60 genera, 700-1,500 species, 2 species native in our 4 counties. Example: California Fremontia.

Carrot, *Apiaceae*
Annual, biennial, or perennial sometimes with fern like leaves. Many small flowers with 5 petals in umbels. Many members of this family are cultivated for food or spice but some are highly toxic e.g., Poison Hemlock that locally is a non native invasive weed. Worldwide 300 genera, 3,000 species, 80 species native in our 4 counties. Examples: Cow Parsnip, Coastal Angelica.

Deer Fern, *Blechnaceae*
Fern, short creeping to erect. Leaves all alike or of 2 kinds, fertile and sterile; blade deeply pinnately lobed. Worldwide approximately 9 genera, 250 species, 2 species native in our 4 counties. Example: Giant Chain Fern.

Dodder, *Cuscutaceae*
Threadlike annual parasitic vine. Tiny flowers and fruits not noticeable. Worldwide 1 genus, about 150 species, 12 species native in our 4 counties. Example: Salt Marsh Dodder.

Dogbane, *Apocynaceae*
Perennial, sometimes annual, shrub, vine, or tree. Small flowers with 5 petals borne singly or in clusters. Worldwide 150-200 genera, 1,000-2,000 species, 4 species native in our 4 counties. Example: Indianhemp Dogbane.

Dogwood, *Cornaceae*
Mostly trees, shrubs, or woody plants with opposite or whorl like leaves with arcuate veins, usually deciduous. Flowers are regular with 4-5 petals, 4-5 sepals; some have large showy bracts surrounding smaller true flowers clustered in the center. Worldwide 11-12 genera, 100 species, only 1 genus native to North America, 6 species native in our 4 counties. Example: Pacific Dogwood.

Evening Primrose, *Onagraceae*
Usually annual or perennial herb, rarely shrubs or trees. Flowers often showy, 4 sepals and 4 petals mostly separate, united into tube at base. Worldwide 15-20 genera, 650-675 species, 12 genera in North America, 88 species native in our 4 counties. Examples: Clarkia, Zauschneria, Sun Cup, and Evening Primrose.

Figwort, *Scrophulariaceae*
Mostly annual or perennial herbs, sometimes shrubs, rarely trees. Flowers are often showy, irregular with 4-5 petals united as a tube, usually 2 lipped with 3 lobes down and 2 lobes above. Worldwide 200 genera, 3,000 species, 40 genera in North America, 165 species native in our 4 counties. Some genus have been placed in Orobanchaceae. Example: California Bee Plant.

Flax, *Linaceae*
Mostly annual, some perennial or shrub. Flowers are radially symmetrical, typically in forked cluster. Seed capsules are 5 chambered, like the sections of an orange. Plant supplies fibers for linen and seeds for linseed oil. Worldwide 12-13 genera, 300 species, 2 genera native to North America, 13 species native in our 4 counties. Example: Slender Western Flax.

Four O'Clock, *Nyctaginaceae*
Mostly perennial herbs, shrubs or vines, sometimes small trees. Funnel shaped flowers have 4-5 colored sepals and no petals. Leaves are simple, opposite; pairs often unequal in size. Worldwide 30 genera, 300 species, 15 genera in North America, 6 species native in our 4 counties. Example: Sand Verbena.

Frankenia, *Frankeniaceae*
Perennial, shrub, subshrub, generally from rhizome, mat forming. Leaves are opposite, numerous with pairs oriented perpendicular to neighboring pairs. Worldwide 1 genus, 90 species, 1 species native in our 4 counties. Example: Alkali Heath.

Gentian, *Gentianaceae*
Annual or perennial with distinctive bell or trumpet shaped tubular flowers in branched clusters. Flower parts generally in 4-5: sepals, stamens, and united petals. Worldwide 70-80 genera, 900-1,100 species, 13 genera in North America, 13 species native in our 4 counties. Example: Centaury.

Gooseberry, *Grossulariaceae*
Shrubs with leaves distinctive, palmately lobed, and generally clustered on short, lateral branches, mostly deciduous, forest understory plants. Flowers are regular, bisexual, in racemes, usually pendant, showy. Berries are translucent and edible. Worldwide 1 genus, 120-150 species, 30 species native in our 4 counties. Examples: Hillside Gooseberry (spines), Pink-flowering Currant (spineless).

Gourd, *Cucurbitaceae*
Perennial herb, prostrate or climbing vine with tendrils. Flowers are funnel shaped and form large 3-4 celled often edible fruit. Many genera are economically important. Worldwide 90-100 genera, 700-850 species, 14 genera in North America, 4 species native in our 4 counties. Example: Manroot (non edible).

Grape, *Vitaceae*
Vining woody plants with tendrils and berries. Leaves are wide, lobed, alternate, forming opposite from the tendrils and flowers, deciduous, colorful in fall. The small flowers are regular with 4 or 5 sepals and petals and 4 or 5 stamens. Most have edible leaves, stems, sap, and berries. Worldwide 12 genera, 700 species, including 4 genera in North America, 1 species native in our 4 counties. Example: California Wild Grape.

Grass, *Poaceae*
Perennial or annual monocot. The grasses are wind pollinated, lacking showy petals and sepals. Greatest economic importance of any family as it includes all our cereal grains. Worldwide 650-900 genera, 10,000 species, 178 species native in our 4 counties with many of them perennial bunch grasses. Example: California Fescue.

Heath, *Ericaceae*
Shrubs and trees, some annuals and perennials. Flowers are mostly red, pink, or white, bell or lantern shaped. Leaves usually alternate, simple, often leathery, evergreen. Numerous species cultivated as ornamentals or source of edible fruits. Worldwide 50-125 genera, 3,000-3,500 species, about 25 genera native to North America, 72 species native in our 4 counties. Examples: Madrone, Manzanita, Salal, Rhododendron, and Azalea.

Honeysuckle, *Caprifoliaceae*
Perennial, shrub, or vine. Flower has 5 petals formed into a slender tube flared at the end, usually in branched or forked clusters. Leaves are opposite, simple or pinnately divided, pithy stems. Berries usually paired or in clusters. Worldwide 12-15 genera, 400-450 species, 7 genera native to North America, 17 species native in our 4 counties. Examples: Honeysuckle, Twinberry, Elderberry, Sugarstick.

Horsetail, *Equisetaceae*
Stiff, erect, fertile and non fertile types, ridged lengthwise, and hollow. Infertile stalks with linear branches in whorls at spaced nodes along the stem. The fertile stalk produces a cone like structure at the top covered in spore producing scales. Sometimes called Scouring Rush due to high silica content. Worldwide 1 genus, 15-23 species, 5 species native in our 4 counties with most in wet places. Example: Horsetail.

Iris, *Iridaceae*
Long lived perennial growing from bulb, corm, or rhizome. Leaves are tough, blade like, simple, overlapping one another fan like at base. Flowers with parts in multiples of 3. Unique characteristic of family is 2 dried, papery bracts below each fully expanded flower. Worldwide 70-80 genera, 1,500 species, 10 species native in our 4 counties. Examples: Irises, Blue-eyed Grass, and Yellow-eyed Grass.

Laurel, *Lauraceae*
Shrub or tree, evergreen, aromatic. Flowers are small yellow or greenish with deeply lobed petals, fruit an olive like drupe. Worldwide about 45 genera, 2,200 species, 1 species native in our 4 counties. Example: California Bay, susceptible to Sudden Oak Death and may spread the disease to oaks.

Leadwort, *Plumbaginaceae*
Perennial herbs or shrubs with leaves often in basal rosettes. Flowers are small, numerous, in heads, dry spikes, or branched clusters. Often found near the sea on salty soil. Worldwide 12-19 genera, 400-775 species, 2 native seaside species in our 4 counties. Examples: Sea Lavender and Sea Thrift.

Lily, *Liliaceae*
Mostly perennial monocot, sometimes woody, grows from bulb, corm, or rhizome. Flowers are showy, single, or sometimes in branched clusters, radial sepals and petals are usually identical. Worldwide 270-300 genera, 3,700-4,600 species, about 75 genera in North America, 138 species native in our 4 counties. Examples: Leopard Lily, Fawn Lily, Golden Fairy Lantern, Trillium, and Death Camas.

Loasa, *Loasaceae*
Annual or perennial herb, with rough, hooked or stinging hairs. Flowers are showy, 2-4 inches in diameter, generally in branched clusters. Worldwide 15 genera, 200-250 species, 5 species native in our 4 counties. Example: Blazing Star.

Mallow, *Malvaceae*
Annuals, perennials, shrubs. Flower has numerous stamens united to form a distinct, funnel shaped tube around the pistil. Worldwide 75-100 genera, 1,500-2,000 species, 27 genera in North America many in warm climates, 31 species native in our 4 counties. Example: Checker Mallow.

Maple, *Aceraceae*
Shrubs, trees, deciduous, grows in shady woods or riparian. Flowers are catkins; winged seeds in pairs. Popular in gardens, fall color. Worldwide 2 genera, 120 species, 3 species native in our 4 counties. Example: Bigleaf Maple.

Meadowfoam, *Limnanthaceae*
Annual, found in vernal pools and other moist places. Delicate spring flowers are white, yellow, or white and yellow, translucent, borne on slender stalks. Small family of 2 genera, 10-14 species all restricted to North America, primarily California, 14 species native in our 4 counties. Examples: White Meadowfoam, Snowy Meadowfoam and the endangered Sebastopol Meadowfoam.

Milkweed, *Asclepiadaceae*
Perennial or annual with simple leaves, opposite or in whorls. Crown like flowers, radially symmetrical with 5 sepals, 5 petals reflexed or spreading. Worldwide 50-250 genera, 2,000-3,000 species, 9 species native in our 4 counties. Example: various Milkweed.

Milkwort, *Polygalaceae*
Mostly annual or perennial, some shrub, tree, or vine. Stems are milky. Flowers are irregular, bisexual, with 5 sepals, 3 green and 2 petal like, and 3 petals with the lower petal often fringed. Generally 8 stamens fuse into a tube that splits open. Worldwide 13-18 genera, 800 species, 2 genera found in North America, 2 species native in our 4 counties. Example: Milkwort.

Mint, *Lamiaceae*
Annual, perennial, or shrub. Distinctly square stalk with usually aromatic leaves. Flowers have 5 petals united in tube like shape often with upper and lower lips. Many species cultivated for herbs and oils. Worldwide 180-200 genera, 3,200-5,500 species, 50 genera in North America, 49 species native in our 4 counties. Examples: Yerba Buena, Pitcher Sage, and Chia.

Mock-orange, *Philadelphaceae*
Loosely branched shrub or subshrub. Flowers white, with 4-7 sepals, 4-7 petals, often many stamens. Worldwide 7 genera, 130 species, 1 species is Idaho's state flower, 3 species native in our 4 counties. Example: Modesty.

Morning-glory, *Convolvulaceae*
Perennial or annual, generally twining or trailing, some parasitic, some shrubs, trees. Flowers are commonly handsome with 5 petals united into tubular, or funnel shape, some have a star pattern inside. Leaves are simple, alternate. Worldwide 50 genera, 1,000-1,650 species, 10 genera in North America, 27 species of Morning Glory native to our 4 counties. Example: Western Morning Glory.

Mustard, *Brassicaceae*
Perennial or annual. Leaves simple, sometimes pinnately compound, often edible or medicinal. Flowers have 4 petals arranged as a cross or X, with 4 tall, 2 short stamens. Worldwide 300-375 genera, 3,000-3,200 species, 55 genera in North America, 126 species native in our 4 counties. Example: Wallflower.

Nettle, *Urticaceae*
Herbaceous annual or perennial, shrubs to tropical trees, sometimes covered with stinging hairs on the foliage, stems and other plant parts. Flowers are greenish, found in string like clusters at the nodes. Stems are often brittle, sometimes fibrous, square, or ridged. Worldwide 45-50 genera, 550-700 species, 5 species native in our 4 counties. Example: Stinging Nettle.

Night Shade, *Solanaceae*
Perennials or annuals, shrubs, vines, or rarely trees. Leaves are generally alternate with colorless juice. Flowers have 5 united sepals, 5 united petals and usually 5 stamens. Berries or seed capsules have 2 cells or chambers. Many of our favorite foods come from this family, such as potatoes and tomatoes. Some plants are poisonous. Worldwide 75-85 genera, 2,300-3,000 species, 13 genera in North America, 12 species native in our 4 counties. Example: Purple Night Shade.

Oak, *Fagaceae*
Mostly trees, some shrubs, some deciduous either winter or drought, some evergreen. Leaves are alternate and leaf margin is entire, lobed, toothed, or serrated. Small flowers are in slender, drooping catkins. Fruits are acorns eaten by a variety of wildlife. Numerous hybrids between California Oak species. Worldwide 7 genera, 900 species, 21 species native in our 4 counties. Examples: California Black Oak, Coast Live Oak.

Olive, *Oleaceae*
Shrubs and trees, deciduous or evergreen, leaves simple or pinnate. Flowers have 4 united sepals, 4 united petals, 2 stamens - a rare combination. Plant typically produces a pair of winged seeds, a berry or fleshy edible fruit. Worldwide 25-29 genera, 600-900 species, 5 genera found in North America, 2 species native in our 4 counties. Example: Oregon Ash.

Orchid, *Orchidaceae*
Perennial from rhizomes, often with complicated, beautiful flowers; many twist one half turn during development making the flower bottom the flower top. The lower petal is often lip like. Often distinguished during flowering by inferior ovary elongating into a seed capsule. The largest family, worldwide 735-1,000 genera, 18,000-20,000 species, 88 genera and 285 species in North America, 27 species native in our 4 counties. Examples: California Lady's Slipper, Calypso Orchid, and Stream Orchid.

Pea, *Fabaceae*
Annuals, perennials, shrubs and trees with fruits in distinctive pods and often pinnate leaves. Flowers in northern latitudes are known for banner wing keel structure formed by 5 petals. Legumes, such as peas and beans, are a major food source. Third largest family, worldwide 600-650 genera, 8,000-13,000 species, 177 species native in our 4 counties. Examples: Lupine, Clover, Pea, Redbud.

Peony, *Paeoniaceae*
Perennial herbs, sometimes subshrubs. Large fragrant flowers, compound leaves; roots found generally in fleshy clusters. There are many hybrids and cultivated forms, often with doubled flowers. Worldwide 1-2 genera, 30-34 species, 2 species in North America, 1 species native in our 4 counties. Example: Western Peony.

Phlox, *Polemoniaceae*
Annual or perennial leafy plant or subshrub, most with narrow leaves, some prickly. Flowers are delicate, showy with 5 united petals, usually twisted in the bud stage. Flowers often form a slender tube at the base with a flat dish like face. Worldwide 18-19 genera, 300-320 species, 93 species native in our 4 counties. Examples: Phlox and Gilia.

Pine, *Pinaceae*
Mostly trees, some shrubs of great commercial value. Simple evergreen leaves, generally alternate, have two forms: needles (mostly) and scales. Needles persist for several years in healthy trees. Cones generally mature in 1-3 years. More species than any other tree in California. Worldwide 10 genera, 193 species, 26 species native in our four counties. Example: Douglas-fir.

Pink, *Caryophyllaceae*
Annual or perennial with swollen nodes on stems, leaves usually opposite, sometimes whorled. Flowers usually 5 petals fringed or toothed ("pinked") at tips. Worldwide 75-85 genera, 2,000-2,400 species, 20 genera in North America, 43 species native in our 4 counties. Examples: Field Chickweed and Indian Pink.

Pipevine, *Aristolochiaceae*
Perennial from rhizome, woody vine, ground cover, or shrub with interesting tubular flowers and parts in 3's. Worldwide 10 genera, 600 species, 2 species native in our 4 counties. Examples: Dutchman's Pipe and Wild Ginger.

Plantain, *Plantaginaceae*
Annual or perennial, low green leafy rosettes with inconspicuous greenish flowers on slender stalks. Leaves are simple with parallel major veins. Produces lidded seed capsules. Worldwide 3 genera, 270 species, 2 genera in North America, 8 species of Plantain native in our 4 counties. Example: Dwarf Plantain.

Polypody, *Polypodiaceae*
Perennial fern growing in soil or among rocks, with long creeping rhizome, blade pinnate to deeply pinnately lobed. Worldwide 46 genera, 650 species, 4 species native in our 4 counties. Number of genera and species depend on treatment. Example: California Polypody.

Poppy, *Papaveraceae*
Annual or perennial, occasionally shrub or small tree. Flowers have 4, 6, or more separate petals, sometimes in 2 unlike pairs; bud is often wrinkled. Sepals 2-4 fall as buds open. Worldwide 26-40 genera, 200-400 species, 13 genera in North America, 21 species native in our 4 counties. Examples: California Poppy, Bleeding Hearts, Cream Cups, and Bush Poppy.

Primrose, *Primulaceae*
Leafy annual or perennial with showy single flowers or flower clusters. Flower parts are usually in 5s. Petals are fat in the middle and taper to a point with stamens aligned in the middle of each petal. Worldwide 25-28 genera, 600-800 species, 11 genera in North America, 9 species native in our 4 counties. Example: Shooting Star.

Purslane, *Portulacaceae*
Annual or perennial, low, smooth yellow green or dark green succulent plants, many preferring intense sunlight. Flowers are regular, bisexual, usually with 2 sepals; plants produce numerous seeds. Worldwide 19-20 genera, 400-580 species, 9 genera native to North America, 38 species native in our 4 counties. Examples: Red Maids, Pussy Paws, and Miner's Lettuce.

Rose, *Rosaceae*
Annuals, perennials, shrubs or trees, some with prickly stems. Flowers are regular with 5 sepals and 5 petals and numerous stamens often in multiples of 5. Many species have oval, serrated leaves. A family that has many introduced species in nurseries. Worldwide 100 genera, 3,000 species, about 50 genera are found in North America, 91 species native in our 4 counties. Examples: Roses, Strawberry, and Toyon.

Rush, *Juncaceae*
Annual or perennial monocot, generally from rhizomes, typically found in seeps, marshes, wet meadows. Erect, grasslike leaves are stiff, commonly cylindrical. Worldwide 9 genera, 325-400 species, 2 genera found in North America, 40 species native in our 4 counties. Example: Salt Rush.

Saxifrage, *Saxifragaceae*
Perennials from rhizomes, leaves usually in basal rosette with flowers on erect stem, singly or in panicles. Flowers with 5 sepals, 5-10 petals and 5-10 stamens all attached to the edge of a cup like flower base with 2-3 styles. Worldwide 30-40 genera, 580-700 species, 20 genera in North America, 32 species native in our 4 counties. Examples: Alumroot, Woodland Star, Saxifrage, and Fringe Cups.

Sedge, *Cyperaceae*
Mostly perennial, sometimes annual grass like monocot of wet places. Often with sharp edged, 3 sided stems. Flowers, cluster of spikelets in axil of bract along stem. Leaves and stems are woven into baskets and mats. A source of papyrus in Egypt. Worldwide 70-110 genera, 3,600-4,000 species, 24 genera in North America, 120 species native in our 4 counties. Example: Naked Sedge.

Silk-tassel, *Garryaceae*
Shrub or small tree, leaves are simple, opposite, leathery, wavy edged, flat to concave or convex, evergreen. Flowers in hanging catkins. Species confined to western North America with 1 genus, 14 species, 5 species native in our 4 counties. Example: Coast Silk Tassel.

Spicebush, *Calycanthaceae*
Shrub, deciduous or evergreen, leaves simple, opposite, aromatic. Large, radial flower on end of branch. Worldwide 3 genera, 6 species worldwide, 1 species native in our 4 counties. Example: Spicebush.

Spurge, *Euphorbiaceae*
Annual or perennial, some with colorful bracts. Male and female flowers are not showy and appear separately on the same plant (monoecious). Milky sap may irritate eyes and mouth. Worldwide 300 genera, 7,500 species, about 25 genera are found in North America with many being weeds, 8 species native in our 4 counties. Example: Turkey Mullein.

St. John's Wort, *Hypericaceae*
Annual or perennial, shrub, rarely tree. Flowers are generally yellow gold, with many stamens. Leaves are simple, opposite, often with dark glands or translucent dots. An invasive weed, the narrow leafed Klamath Weed, *Hypericum perforatum*, is used by herbalists as an anti depressant. Worldwide 8-10 genera, 356-400 species, 3 species native in our 4 counties. Examples: Tinker's Penny and Gold Wire.

Stonecrop, *Crassulaceae*
Succulent annual or perennial, sometimes small shrub. Leaves often are in rosettes, waxy, opposite or alternate, simple or pinnate. Small flowers typically have 4-5 (sometimes up to 30) sepals, petals and many stamens attached at base of 3 to several pistils. Worldwide 25-35 genera, 900-1,550 species, 9 genera in North America, 21 species native in our 4 counties. Examples: Dudleya and Sedum.

Sumac, *Anacardiaceae*
Shrubs, sometimes vining, with 3 lobed or pinnate leaves and red or white berries. Flowers are 5 petaled, small, in raceme or panicle. Worldwide 70 genera, 850 species, 2 species native in our 4 counties. Example: Poison Oak. Touching or burning all parts of Poison Oak should be avoided, but enjoy its fall color at a distance.

Sunflower, *Asteraceae*
Perennial or annual herb, shrub, or vine. Leaves simple to compound, alternate to opposite. Tiny specialized flowers tightly clustered in a single flower head usually include both disk and ray flowers (daisy type), or either, producing many seeds. Many species produce edible seeds, greens, or oil. One of two largest families, worldwide 920-1,100 genera, 19,000-20,000 species, 380 species native in our 4 counties. Examples: Goldfields, Aster, Mugwort, Coyote Brush, Gumplant, California Dandelion, Goldenrod, and various Sunflowers.

Valerian, *Valerianaceae*
Leafy annual or perennial, often strongly scented plants with small flowers in dense clusters. Leaves are basal and opposite. Flowers have tiny spurs, sepals are inconspicuous, typically produces one seeded fruit. Roots have pungent odor. Worldwide 13-17 genera, 300-400 species, 3 genera are found in North America, 10 species native in our 4 counties. Example: Plectritis.

Violet, *Violaceae*
Perennial or annual with distinctive, irregular, open, pansy like flowers. Flower parts on plan of 5s with 2 upper petals, 2 at the sides, and a lower single petal. A popular family for the garden. Worldwide 15-22 genera, 600-900 species, 2 genera are found in North America, 27 species native in our 4 counties. Examples: Redwood Violet, Western Dog Violet, Johnny Jump-up, and Western Heart's Ease.

Water Lily, *Nymphaeaceae*
Perennial aquatic plants with large floating leaves. Solitary flowers on long stalk and 3 to numerous petals. Worldwide about 7 genera, 68 species and 4 genera in North America, 1 species native in our 4 counties. Example: Yellow Pond-Lily.

Waterleaf, *Hydrophyllaceae*
Most annual or perennial, few are shrubs, generally bristly or hairy. Flowers typically small with 5 parts, often clustered along one side of branch, often blue. Stalks curl over like scorpion tail. Worldwide 20 genera, 250-270 species, 16 genera native to North America, 69 species native in our 4 counties. Examples: Phacelia, Baby Blue-Eyes, and Yerba Santa.

Water-Plantain, *Alismataceae*
Usually fresh water aquatic, annual or perennial, with milky latex sap. Leaves are basal, simple, palmately veined, sometimes floating. Flowers have 3 petals. Worldwide 12 genera, 75-100 species, 8 species native in our 4 counties. Example: Broad-leaf Arrowhead.

Wood Fern, *Dryopteridaceae*
Perennial ferns found in forest soil or rock crevices. Rhizome short creeping, sub erect, or erect. Blades 1-4 pinnate. Worldwide about 60 genera, > 1,000 species, 13 species native in our 4 counties. Examples: Wood Fern, Western Lady Fern, and Sword Fern.

Wood Sorrel, *Oxalidaceae*
Small, perennial herb with alternate, shamrock leaves. Flower parts in 5s. Worldwide 8 genera, 575-950 species, 1 genus native in North America, 4 species native in our 4 counties. Example: Redwood Sorrel.

Yew, *Taxaceae*
Evergreen trees of conifer form with stiff, simple, needlelike leaves not in bundles. Male and female flowers on separate plants (dioecious) and red or green cup shaped fruits. Worldwide 5 genera, 20 species, 2 genera native to North America, 2 species native in our 4 counties. Examples: Pacific Yew and California Nutmeg.

White

Broadleaf Arrowhead

Sagittaria latifolia
Water Plantain Family,
Alismataceae

Blooming in late summer, this plant with distinctive arrowhead shaped leaves can be found near still water ponds and ephemeral streams. The three white petals are in whorls of three on leafless stems.

California Indians ate the cooked tubers. Various parts of plant were used for medicinal purposes.

Broadleaf Arrowhead is an aquatic plant which is happiest in a bog or very near the water's margin, in sun to part sun. This plant can be invasive wherever there is enough water.

Jul–Sep ● Ma, So, Na
30–120 cm, 1–4 ft

Broadleaf Arrowhead ●

Wavyleaf Soap Plant

Chlorogalum pomeridianum, var. *pomeridianum*
Lily Family, *Liliaceae*

In fall, you'll find small bundles of bristly fibers surrounding the bulbs of this useful perennial. Winter brings basal rosettes of linear leaves 20-70 cm, 8-25 in, long with wavy margins. In summer loose clusters of flowers formed by six spidery looking petals in white to pink with a green mid vein will bloom, but not until late afternoon. Pollinated by moths, the flowers seem to float in the moonlight of the woodlands.

The bristly fibers make brushes and small brooms. Soap, shampoo, and glue are made from crushed roots. Native Americans ate the roasted bulbs.

This deciduous native with tall stalks of delicate flowers adds evening interest to the garden.

May–Jul ● Ma, So, Na, Me
.6–2 m, 2–7 ft

Wavyleaf Soap Plant

Hooker's Fairybell

Disporum hookeri
Lily Family, *Liliaceae*

This charming perennial grows from rhizomes in shady woods away from the coast. The stems have few branches with irregularly curled hairs. Leaves are alternate, oval to lance shaped with pointed tips and prominent veins. They are slightly hairy on the upper surface and margins. The creamy white to greenish white bell shaped flowers are clustered in two's hanging from the end of the branch. Fruit is a lemon yellow to orange red berry.

A similar plant is Largeflower Fairybell with, as the name implies, larger flowers.

Mar–May ● Ma, So, Na, Me
30–90 cm, 1–3 ft

Hooker's Fairybell

Largeflower Fairybell

Disporum smithii
Lily Family, *Liliaceae*

A pretty perennial favoring shady woods near the coast, but is sometimes found inland. Flowers are creamy white to greenish white, cylindrical, and usually clustered with 1-7 flowers hanging from the tip of a branch. Fruits are lemon yellow to orange red, egg shaped and often hairy. The stems have few branches and irregularly curled hairs. Leaves are alternate oval to lance

shaped with pointed tips and prominent veins. They are slightly hairy on the upper surface and margins.

This plant is similar to Hooker's Fairybell which is found away from the coast.

Mar–Jun ● Ma, So, Na, Me
30–90 cm, 1–3 ft

Largeflower Fairybell

False Lily of the Valley
Maianthemum dilatatum
Lily Family, *Liliaceae*

Although uncommon, this lovely plant sometimes carpets damp, shaded embankments. The very attractive heart shaped leaves emerge in the spring and spread in a widening patch, creeping underground by rhizomes. Leaves grow two on a stem with prominent parallel veins. Four petals form dainty white flowers that bloom in a row along a tiny stalk. They have a faint, sweet scent. Flowers are followed by green gold colored berries that deepen to bright red by fall.

Native Americans ate the berries fresh or dried.

May–Jun ● Ma, So, Me
10–40 cm, 4–15 in

False Lily of the Valley

Star Lily
Zigadenus fremontii
Lily Family, *Liliaceae*

On rocky outcrops, dry, grassy or wooded slopes you are very likely to find this native perennial in early spring. The single, large, showy flower spike with a profusion of yellowish, star shaped flowers is quite appealing. Each flower has six petals that spread out from the flower center. Petals are greenish at the base and subtly veined. Six stamens wave invitingly from the flower center. This plant has linear, basal leaves.

All parts of this plant are **poisonous**, hence, another common name of Death Camas.

Mar–Apr ● Ma, So, Na, Me
10–80 cm, 4–32 in

Star Lily

Fringed Corn Lily
Veratrum fimbriatum
Lily Family, *Liliaceae*

The frilly white flowers of this rare native make it well worth a search despite its limited distribution. Infrequently found in wet meadows and openings in

north coast forests and coastal scrub. The foliage is interesting for its large, clasping, egg shaped leaves with parallel veins that give rise to a sturdy, erect flower stalk. Half way up the stalk, opposite flower carrying stalks emerge. On each of these there are many ball shaped flower buds or fragrant flowers growing in an erect cluster. Each flower is formed of six white petals with fringed, frilly edges, two lobes, and two greenish yellow spots near the lace like edge of the petal.

Jul–Oct ● So, Me
1–2 m, 3–6 ft

False Solomon's Seal

Smilacina racemosa
Lily Family, *Liliaceae*

This pretty perennial with lovely green foliage and plumes of small white flowers is common to our shady woods. The leaves are long, alternate, and egg shaped with prominent parallel veins. They clasp graceful arching stems that end in branched clusters of more than 20 small white to cream colored flowers. Each tiny flower is formed by six petals. The frothy plumes and green foliage are quite impressive.

Star Solomon's Seal, *Smilacina stellata*, is similar but smaller, and the terminal floral clusters are not branched.

Both False and Star Solomon's Seal are lovely deciduous perennials for the shade garden or containers.

Mar–May ● Ma, So, Na, Me
30–90 cm, 1–3 ft

Beargrass
Xerophyllum tenax
Lily Family, *Liliaceae*

A striking perennial that is easy to spot on open dry ridges and slopes during its long summer blooming season. Tall stalks of many small, sweet scented flowers rise from olive colored grass clumps demanding attention. Each flower is white to cream and formed of six petals. Dense clusters of flowers blooming from the lower level up, create a tight club like bundle of buds at the top of the floral stalk. Tough wiry, grass like leaves grow in a basal clump. They have toothed margins, and clasp around the stem.

Beargrass is fire resistant and one of the first plants to emerge after a fire.

May–Aug ● Ma, So, Na, Me
30–150 cm, 1–5 ft

Beargrass

Chaparral Lily
Lilium rubescens
Lily Family, *Liliaceae*

This rare perennial of dry, wooded ridges, and slopes has white trumpets speckled with maroon spots. The flower turns a dark pink purple as it ages. Each flower is formed of six petals shaped into an upturned trumpet. The flowers are very fragrant and this may be the way you will find them. The

lance shaped leaves with wavy margins grow in groups of 3-13 whorls along the flower stem.

Also known as Redwood Lily.

Jun–Jul ● So, Na, Me
60–150 cm, 2–5 ft

Chaparral Lily

California Fawn Lily
Erythronium californicum
Lily Family, *Liliaceae*

Fawn Lilies have been called the soul of spring, and this beautiful lily is exemplar. On its straight erect stem it is found in open areas of the woods and on brushy slopes. The flowers are white with a greenish yellow base and a ring of yellow, orange, or brown. They droop from short, greenish red stems and grow in clusters of 1-10 flowers in a raceme. The six narrow petals that form the flowers curl backward reminding one of the flying wings of a French nun's habit. Fawn spotted leaves are 7-15 cm, 4-7 in, long. This endemic is a favorite plant of all who are lucky to find its colonies.

California Fawn Lily

A similar plant is St. Helena Fawn Lily, *E. helenae*, a rare plant.

A good addition in the shade for stream side gardens. Purchase bulbs from a reputable nursery.

Mar–Apr ● So, Na, Me
15–30 cm, 6–12 in

California Corn Lily
Veratrum californicum var. *californicum*
Lily Family, *Liliaceae*

This broad leaved perennial grows from thick, fibrous rootstocks on the banks of streams or in wet meadows. It looks very much like a corn plant with its large, egg shaped, parallel veined, and often pleated leaves. They clasp very thick stems in alternate formation. Numerous white or greenish flowers grow on branching, terminal clusters. Flowers are formed of six petals with smooth edges and a green v shaped spot at the base. The fruits are three chambered capsules that contain numerous brown, winged, flat seeds.

This plant is toxic to some animals.

Jul–Sep ● Me
1–2 m, 3–6 ft

California Corn Lily ●

Coast Range Mariposa Lily
Calochortus vestae
Lily Family, *Liliaceae*

This graceful perennial bulb with its 2-6 large bowl shaped flowers has intri-cate petal markings that add great beauty to the flower. Flowers are commonly white but sometimes pink or purple. Each flower has three, wedge shaped petals marked with a red brown blotch in a pale yellow zone with smears of brown and yellow from the base of the petal slightly upward. The leaves are linear, basal and somewhat long. Favoring clay soil in mixed ever-green forests you will find this plant in three of our counties.

Hummingbirds and butterflies collect the nectar and wildlife eat the seed pods.

Coast Range Mariposa Lily

May–Jul ● So, Na, Me
30–50 cm, 12–18 in

Superb Mariposa Lily
Calochortus superbus
Lily Family, *Liliaceae*

"Mariposa" means "butterfly," and the exceptional flower of this gorgeous pe-rennial bulb deserves the comparison to such flitting jewels. Three large petals in white, to yellow or lavender form a cup shaped flower graced with intricate designs. Petals are wedge or heart shaped and come to a subtle point at their

tips. Each petal has a chevron shaped bright yellow zone with a small maroon wedge near its center. Below the col-orful marking is a row of tiny short hairs near the flower's nectary. The leaves are basal and linear. Look for this lovely treasure on open grassland and woodland.

May–Jul ● Ma, So, Na, Me
40–60 cm, 16–24 in

Superb Mariposa Lily

Common Muilla
Muilla maritima
Lily Family, *Liliaceae*

The perky upright flowers of this spring blooming perennial have leaves that are linear and sometimes quite long, ranging from 10-60 cm, 4-24 in. Flowers grow in an umbel of 4-20 flowers. Each flower has six narrow white to greenish petals with a brownish mid rib stretching out from the flower center where the pistil is prominent. Only occasionally found and favoring coastal sage scrub, chaparral, and woodlands, this shy native avoids our northern most county.

Muillas resemble some members of the onion genus, *Allium*. *Muilla* is actually *Allium* spelled backwards. An easy way to tell them apart is that *Muilla* has no onion odor.

Mar–Jun ● Ma, So, Na
15–60 cm, 6–24 in

Common Muilla

Wild Hyacinth
Triteleia hyacinthina
Lily Family, *Liliaceae*

Common in low, moist meadows, vernal pools, along streams, and occasionally on drier slopes, this little beauty has a green mid rib vein on each of its petals. Small white flowers grow on short stalks and are grouped in an umbel on an erect stem. Each flower has six petals and six true stamens. Foliage is

basal with 2-3 narrowly lance shaped stem leaves which are often withered when the flowers bloom.

Long-ray Brodiaea, *Triteleia peduncularis*, is similar but has longer stalks and pure white flowers with no green midrib on the petals.

A good garden plant that favors sun to partial shade and likes containers.

Apr–Aug ● Ma, So, Na, Me
15–60 cm, 6–24 in

Wild Hyacinth

Phantom Orchid

Phantom Orchid

Cephalanthera austiniae
Orchid Family,
Orchidaceae

This green to ghost white, elusive orchid makes a striking find in the deep shade of conifer forests. Growing only in the decomposing humus of the forest floor, this saprophytic perennial contains no chlorophyll, and survives through a symbiotic relationship with fungi. The three sepals and two petals form a typical orchid like lip. There is no color in the flower parts other than a dark yellow splash on the lip. The leaves have been reduced to membranous sheathing bracts along the flowering stem.

May ● Ma, So, Na, Me
30–61 cm, 1–2 ft

Rattlesnake Plantain

Goodyera oblongifolia
Orchid Family,
Orchidaceae

Look for this small, delicate plant along trails on dry forest floors. It is not very common but the stout, shiny blue green leaves with a prominent white stripe along the midrib may attract your attention; they look like the skin pattern of rattlesnakes. Oblong to elliptical, the leaves form a basal rosette. They are large compared to the miniature white green flowers growing along a thin stalk. One fused petal and three sepals form a hood like lipped orchid flower.

California Indians used the plant sap as a chewing gum.

Jun–Aug ● Ma, So, Me
18–35 cm, 7–14 in

Rattlesnake Plantain

Lady's Tresses

Spiranthes romanzoffiana
Orchid Family, *Orchidaceae*

Common to a variety of moist to wet habitats, the distinctive flowers of this late blooming orchid make it easy to identify. This image was taken in February by a plant that didn't know its bloom time! The upper sepal and lateral petals are fused into small, violin shaped flowers with a down curving lip. The small, white, translucent flowers twist in three vertical rows to form a dense spiral along an erect flower spike, reminding one very much of a lady's braided hair. Long grasslike, linear, basal leaves wither by bloom time.

The name refers to Count Romanzoff, Russian patron of botany.

Jun–Aug ● Ma, So, Na, Me
8–30 cm, 3–12 in

Lady's Tresses

Cream Cups

Platystemon californicus
Poppy Family, *Papaveraceae*

In open grassy clay or sandy places, chaparral and burns, this lovely annual scents the air with a delicate sweet perfume. The grey green leaves are opposite, entire, lance to linear in a basal cluster. The solitary flowers sit on almost leafless stems with many long hairs. They burst open from pods formed by three hairy sepals. Each flower has many stamens and six showy white to cream colored petals which are bright yellow at the tips.

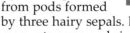

Ideal for seeding in a wildflower garden, this plant favors full sun and dry soil, although it grows well in any well drained garden.

Mar–May ● Ma, So, Na, Me
10–30 cm, 4–12 in

Cream Cups

Milkmaids...
a bit plain
and unadorned
but you try rising
before everyone else

Milkmaids

Cardamine californica
Mustard Family, *Brassicaceae*

Its name evoking the image of blonde, pig tailed, young women, the little white to pink, four petaled bloom may not live up to its billing. However, this early bloomer of shady, moist spots invokes the promise of approaching springtime. A solitary rounded leaf marks this plant from the first fall rains until the stem develops. One of the earliest blooming plants, Milkmaids may be found in canyons, woods, coastal scrub, and grasslands.

Feb–May ● Ma, So, Na, Me
10–40 cm, 4–15 in

Milkmaids

Watercress

Rorippa nasturtium–aquaticum
Mustard Family, *Brassicaceae*

Watercress, as the name implies, is found in moist areas along slow moving streams and woodland meadows. The blooms are four petaled, tiny white flowers in terminal clusters. Stems are sprawling and succulent like with compound leaves.

There seems to be confusion as to whether Watercress is a native plant. However, our definitive source, Calfora, lists it as native.

Another name is *Nasturtium officinale*.

Mar–Nov ● Ma, So, Na, Me
30–60 cm, 1–2 ft

Watercress

Lace Pod

Thysanocarpus curvipes
Mustard Family, *Brassicaceae*

An early spring annual, the tiny, white, four petaled flowers with a purple tinge give way in summer to distinctive round pods. The flattened seed is surrounded by a papery margin with thick ribs. The disks decorate the tall stem with its basal, narrow, arrowhead leaves. You will most easily find this native in the grasslands when it is backlit.

Mar–May ● Ma, So, Na, Me
15–90 cm, 6–36 in

Lace Pod

Coast Buckwheat

Eriogonum latifolium
Buckwheat Family, *Polygonaceae*

Look for this hardy perennial in cracks of smooth coastal rock faces, on dry beach sand dunes, or in stony areas. Its pom pom shaped flower clusters are white in summer, turning to rust in late fall. Tiny tubular flowers of six petals may be different colors on the same flower cluster. Leaves are oblong to egg shaped in basal clusters, gray green in summer with white woolly undersides. They turn to orange red in fall.

Native Americans prized this plant for its many medicinal uses. Butterflies seek its nectar and rabbits eat the leaves and flowers.

In coastal gardens this plant survives on sunny, sandy/rocky soil with little attention.

Jun–Sep ● Ma, So, Me
10–70 cm, 4–28 in

Coast Buckwheat

Naked Buckwheat

Eriogonum nudum var. *nudum*
Buckwheat Family, *Polygonaceae*

This curious plant is commonly found in rocky outcrops and dry, open habitats. Tiny white or pale pink flowers are formed of six petals. They grow in a cluster atop a tall, bare, leafless stem. There is a flat basal rosette of dark green, oval leaves. It is the naked stem that gives this plant its name.

Butterflies are particularly attracted to Buckwheat flowers for their nectar.

Jun–Sep ● Ma, So, Na, Me
15–90 cm, 6–36 in

Golden Buckwheat

Golden Buckwheat

Eriogonum luteolum
Buckwheat Family,
Polygonaceae

This somewhat spindly annual plant is common to gravelly, sandy, dry places with excellent drainage and nearly full sun. It is sometimes found on serpentine. The small tubular flowers are composed of six white to rose or yellow petals that grow in a small cluster on nearly leafless branching stems. Leaves are round and generally basal.

Jun–Sep ● Ma, So, Na, Me
15–60 cm, 6–24 in

Vanilla Leaf

Achlys californica
Barberry Family,
Berberidaceae

One may be fortunate to find this delicate flowered Barberry species in shady, moist coastal forests. The very large single leaf is actually in three leaflets with a long stem topped with a cluster of tiny white flowers. The petals are really too small to count, but the multiple flowers do form a spike like cluster on this lovely perennial.

Apr–Jun ● So, Me
25–50 cm, 10–20 in

Vanilla Leaf

Inside-out Flower
Vancouveria planipetala
Barberry Family, *Berberidaceae*

Interestingly, this *Vancouveria* of our Redwood forests is called the "inside out" flower. It was in part due to the 1790's explorations of the Pacific Northwest by George Vancouver that brought the "outside in" to this forested region of the world. This tiny, delicate flower with its swept back petals is in such contrast to its neighbors, the world's tallest trees. The leaf is compound with heart shaped leaflets.

This perennial likes shade and moderate moisture in the garden. An unusual spring blooming flower.

> **May–Jun ● Ma, So, Me**
> **15–60 cm, 6–24 in**

Inside-out Flower

Little Prince's Pine
Chimaphila menziesii
Heath Family, *Ericaceae*

This secretive white blossomed member of the Heath Family is found in the shade of coastal conifers. The common name suggests the ethereal nature of the nodding, five petaled, shiny, pinkish white flowers. They appear to be

miniature crowns waiting to be placed on the prince's head. The lance shaped linear leaves are armed with spikey sharp teeth.

Another common name is Pipsissewa.

> **Jun–Aug ● So, Na, Me**
> **to 15 cm, 6 in**

Little Prince's Pine

Snowy Meadowfoam
Limnanthes douglasii ssp. *nivea*
Meadowfoam Family, *Limnanthaceae*

The very attractive, showy flowers of this native annual justify taking a camera along when hiking. Common to vernally wet places in all four counties, the bowl shaped flower has five petals. Petal color can be pure white or shade from dark cream near the base of the petal to white at the lobed edges. Petals are streaked with purple pink veins like a pin striped suit, and just as chic. Leaves have 5-11 compound like leaflets.

This plant is similar to Common Meadowfoam but the white petals differentiate this plant from the other.

This low growing annual likes water and sun to part shade. It works well in containers, borders, and rock and meadow gardens.

Snowy Meadowfoam

Mar–May ● Ma, So, Na, Me
to 50 cm, 18 in

Sebastopol Meadowfoam
Limnanthes vinculans
Meadowfoam Family, *Limnanthaceae*

This small, multi stemmed endemic has distinctive leaves. The first leaves are narrow and undivided; on the mature plant they are 3-5 undivided leaflets along each side of a stalk. The shape of the leaves distinguishes this plant from others of the *Limnanthes* genus. The flowers are small, white, and bowl shaped with a single flower growing at the end of a stem. They have the pin stripe veining of other Meadowfoams.

This very rare annual is listed as: CNPS 1B.1, state of California as Endangered, Federal Government as Endangered. It is included in the 2004 Draft Vernal Pool Ecosystem Recovery Plan. Quite a listing for such a small plant.

Apr–May ● So, Na
to 30 cm, 12 in

Sebastopol Meadowfoam

Common Meadowfoam

Limnanthes douglasii ssp. *douglasii*
Meadowfoam Family, *Limnanthaceae*

The white and yellow colors of this cheerful spring bloom are common to wet meadows as a low, spreading carpet of fragrant blooms. The flowers are bowl shaped with five petals and pin stripes typical of Meadowfoams, but the petal color is a vivid goldenrod with white on the outer petal. Leaves are linear and irregularly toothed.

The coloration differentiates this plant from the similar Snowy Meadowfoam.

This low growing annual likes water and sun to part shade. It works well in containers, borders, and rock and meadow gardens.

Mar–May ● Ma, So, Na, Me
to 50 cm, 18 in

Common Meadowfoam

Rosy Douglas' Meadowfoam

Limnanthes douglasii ssp. *rosea*
Meadowfoam Family, *Limnanthaceae*

An annual of moist meadows, this plant produces a profusion of fragrant, white, pin striped flowers. The five petaled flowers are bowl shaped with each petal having two lobes and the pin stripe like veins typical of Meadowfoams. But here pinkish veins are in the petals and the entire petal ages to rose. Leaves are linear and irregularly toothed.

Similar to Common Meadowfoam, but the pinkish colored veins differentiate this plant.

A low growing annual that likes water and sun to part shade. It works well in containers, borders, and rock and meadow gardens.

Mar–May ● Me
10–38 cm, 4–15 in

Rosy Douglas' Meadowfoam

Slender Western Flax

Hesperolinon spergulinum
Flax Family, *Linaceae*

This native annual is occasionally found in chaparral, dry slopes, and grav-
eled barrens of serpentine in Sonoma County. The white to pale pink flowers
bloom in early summer on very
low plants. The five very small
petals that form the flower are
generally wide spreading, and
are yellow or white to rose in
color, each with three small
scales at the inner base. Leaves
are alternate, generally thread
like to linear.

Jun–Jul ● So
10–30 cm, 4–12 in

Slender Western Flax

Meadow Chickweed

Cerastium arvense
Pink Family, *Caryophyllaceae*

Though in the Pink Family the five petalled bloom of this perennial of open
spaces is white. The name "pink" is from the pinking shear type edges of the
petals. Appropriately, Meadow Chickweed's broad petals are deeply notched.
Leaves of this perennial are linear.

Some sources consider *C. arvense* an alien, but our definitive source, Calflora, lists it as a native.

Feb–Aug ● Ma, So, Na, Me
5–50 cm, 2–20 in

Meadow Chickweed

Two-eyed Violet

Viola ocellata
Viola Family, *Violaceae*

Two-eyed Violet is a low growing perennial often found among rocks, grassy banks, and serpentine areas of our four counties. A stunning flower, the white petals are detailed with a small purple eye and yellow banding, and the lower lip petal has deep violet veins. This beautiful flower is matched with equally interesting triangle shaped foliage with toothed margins. Look for this charmer in spring and early summer.

Sometimes called Western Heart's Ease, it has a long history of use in medical treatments of chest complaints such as bronchitis and whooping cough, and for skin diseases such as eczema.

Mar–Jun ● Ma, So, Na, Me
5–40 cm, 2–15 in

Narrowleaf Milkweed
Asclepias fascicularis
Milkweed Family, *Asclepiadaceae*

The snapped stem of this native Narrowleaf Milkweed bleeds the typical milky sap, however please don't feel it necessary to test this. Located in dry places, forests, and various habitats, the stalk has whorls of long thin leaves. Stems hold a greenish white or purple flower with five petals reflexed in umbels.

Less showy than Purple Milkweed, Narrowleaf Milkweed is a very valuable host plant for Monarch butterflies, and a nectar source for many native insects.

This milkweed grows in part to full sun in areas with good drainage, and can be cut to the ground in late summer if it starts to look ungainly. It can be invasive.

Jun–Sep ●Ma, So, Na, Me
60–120 cm, 2–4 ft

Narrowleaf Milkweed

Coast Angelica
Angelica hendersonii
Carrot Family, *Apiaceae*

In the coarse soils of coastal sandstone outcrops this stout stemmed perennial can be seen displaying its tight white umbels. The fragrant balls form multiple 13-15 cm, 5-6 in, umbels from a single stalk. Leaves are compound with rounded leaflets and fine toothed.

Similar species are Cow Parsnip and other Angelicas.

A good specimen plant for the garden with interesting foliage. The very large flower cluster is attractive to many beneficial insects. This plant will not do well in the hottest micro climates.

Jun–Aug ● Ma, So, Me
1.2–1.8 m, 4–6 ft

Coast Angelica

Coyote Thistle

Eryngium armatum
Carrot Family, *Apiaceae*

The barefoot hiker of the coastal bluffs will easily find this low growing plant with cream colored blooms in moist prairie areas and seeps. Sharp tipped bracts, which cause slight pain, will bring the obscure plant to one's attention. The low spreading plant has five tiny petals in a cluster with the leaf a basal rosette.

A California endemic, Coyote Thistle grows nowhere else. Also known as Coastal Eryngo.

Although not commonly cultivated, for a coastal garden this would be an interesting plant in the sun with irrigation.

May–Aug ● Ma, So, Na, Me
5–40 cm, 2–16 in

Coyote Thistle

Cow Parsnip

Heracleum lanatum
Carrot Family, *Apiaceae*

The huge, green, maple like leaves of this very tall plant of coastal gullies, grasslands, and forests are alternately attached to a thick hollow stem. The white to cream or rosy flowers are in a large flat topped cluster. This cluster may remind one of cauliflower and is 15-30 cm, 6-12 in, wide. The flowers are wrapped in a tight green sheath before appearing in spring and summer.

Dried stems were sometimes used by California Indians as whistles. Parts

of the plant were used as a vegetable poultice.

Cow Parsnip has great wildlife value and is easily grown from seed. It requires some moisture in summer, and tolerates full sun in cooler areas, part shade in hot climates. Parts of the plant may cause dermatitis.

Mar–Sep ● Ma, So, Na, Me
to 3.7 m, 12 ft

Cow Parsnip

Woolly-fruited Lomatium

Lomatium dasycarpum
Carrot Family, *Apiaceae*

On the dry, exposed ridges of the North Coast Ranges one may find this umbel flower. A member of the carrot family, it may also be discovered on serpentine. Blooms consist of five tiny petals that sometime take on a greenish white hue. The leaf is finely dissected.

Also known as Hog Fennel.

Mar–Jun ● Ma, So, Na, Me
to 60 cm, 2 ft

Woolly-fruited Lomatium

Yampah

Perideridia gairdneri
Carrot Family, *Apiaceae*

On the open slopes of the North Coast Ranges these white umbel flowers can be found decorating the golden hills in late summer. Leaflets are linear to lance shaped on slender stems. Other Yampahs are similar.

Perideridia was the primary pre Columbian larval host for the Anise Swallowtail butterfly.

The seeds from the bloom were combined with other seeds to make Pinole by California Indians. Rootstocks or bulbs were highly prized.

Not commonly cultivated, but is easily adaptable to gardens if given full sun to part shade in very hot areas and adequate water in spring. Too much water in summer may cause root rot.

Jul–Aug ● Ma, So, Na, Me
60–160 cm, 2–5 ft

Yampah

Western Morning Glory
Calystegia occidentalis
Morning-glory Family, *Convolvulaceae*

The family name *Convolvulaceae* comes from the Latin "to entwine" referring to the trailing, twining, convoluted stem. The lovely trumpet shaped white flowers with faint pink bands appear along the sometimes 1 m, 3 ft, long stem. There is considerable variation in the typical arrowhead shaped leaves. With a hand lens one may see fine hairs on the underside of the leaves and along the leaves and stems. This perennial with deep, woody roots blooms on open slopes and chaparral.

There are similar species, one being *C. purpuratus* with white or pinkish flowers and is devoid of hair. Found more commonly along the coast, it is more likely to be trailing on the ground.

**May–Jul ● Ma, So, Na, Me
stem to 1 m, 3 ft**

Western Morning Glory

Hill Morning Glory
Calystegia subacaulis
Morning-glory Family, *Convolvulaceae*

This perennial has the typical Morning Glory five lobed whitish to purplish tinted flower. These bloom in spring and early summer forming low but spreading mats with the actual vine buried underground. Heart shaped leaves are in an almost stemless cluster.

This common native likes dry open areas in the garden and can be a little weedy.

Another member of the Morning-glory Family, Field Bindweed, *C. arvensis*, is a widespread troublesome weed growing in disturbed areas. Leaves are arrowhead shaped with a sharp pointed lobe. The small (1-4 cm, ½-1½") white or pink tinted flowers bloom from Apr-Oct on trailng stems.

**Apr–Jun ● Ma, So, Na, Me
2–20 cm, 1–8 in**

Hill Morning Glory

Evening Snow

Linanthus dichotomus
Phlox Family, *Polemoniaceae*

During the spring a late afternoon hike through drying open meadows and serpentine habitats may treat your senses to this very appealing charmer.

Opening at dusk the white flowers of this low growing annual give the landscape a snowy appearance. The petals form bright white upright trumpet like flowers with five large lobes. The flowers spring up from linear leaves that are low to the ground. These beautiful little surprises are only occasionally found, so enjoy them fully when you come upon them.

A sub species of this plant blooms in the morning, closing at night.

Apr–Jun ● So, Na
5–20 cm, 2–8 in

Evening Snow

Needleleaf Navarretia

Navarretia intertexta
Phlox Family, *Polemoniaceae*

Although the name makes this unusual, low growing annual sound uninviting it is a charming find in open wet areas, vernal pools, and damp meadows. The small white to pale blue flowers look fragile against their "don't touch me" leaves. Each flower has five small petals fused into a tiny upright trumpet surrounding the stamens. Flowers grow in dense clusters among spike leaves

with prongs at their tips. Leaves emerge from brown stems with white hairs. The sharp contrast of the fragile beauty of the flowers against the needle like leaves makes this plant very interesting.

May–Jul ● Ma, So, Na, Me
8–28 cm, 3–11 in

Needleleaf Navarretia

Imbricate Phacelia

Phacelia imbricata
Waterleaf Family, *Hydrophyllaceae*

This interesting native perennial with its curious flowers is commonly found in dry, rocky places. The stems, flower buds, and foliage are covered with dense, gray hair. The leaves are mostly basal and compound with pairs of lateral, sharply pointed segments and prominent veins. In bud the flowers appear as dense hairy coils, like curled up green caterpillars. The small white to lavender flowers are cylinders or bells with long stamens sticking out well beyond the petals. Each flower looks like a little round head with antennae waving above.

Insects are attracted to the fuzzy white flowers of this plant.

Apr–Jun ● Ma, So, Na, Me
30–60 cm, 1–2 ft

White Baby Blue Eyes
Nemophila menziesii var. *atomaria*
Waterleaf Family, *Hydrophyllaceae*

On coastal bluffs or grassy slopes you'll find this lovely white flower sprinkled in spring floral carpets. Low growing and long blooming, these very pretty flowers are enjoyed from a distance, but even more so close at hand. Five petals form a very attractive bowl shaped white flower with radiating lines of black dots, often with a faint blue tint in the petals. Green, compound, lobed leaves set off the flowers to fine advantage.

This pretty annual likes part sun to shade and does well in containers.

Feb–Jun ● Ma, So, Na, Me
10–30 cm, 4–12 in

White Baby Blue Eyes

Popcorn Flower
Plagiobothrys nothofulvus
Forget-me-not Family,
Boraginaceae

The scientific name, *Plagiobothrys nothofulvus*, is truly a mouthful. It is referring to the tiny nutlet of this plant of coastal grasslands. But one may think of a mouthful of tiny white popped corn due to the five petals pinwheeled in a coiled cluster. The stem and rosette of basal linear leaves are covered with fine reddish yellow hairs.

There are similar *Plagiobothrys* and they are difficult to separate, typically needing a "nutlet."

Mar–May ● Ma, So, Na, Me
15–60 cm, 6–24 in

Popcorn Flower

Small-flowered Nightshade

Solanum americanum
Night Shade Family, *Solanaceae*

Blooming from spring to late fall, this plant grows in moist woods and thickets, pastures, roadsides, and disturbed ground. The small pretty flowers are typically white and grow in a drooping umbel of about five flowers. The five petals have pointed lobes, either spreading or reflexed, and sometimes shades of purple or blue. The leaves seem large in relation to the small flower. They are egg shaped or triangular with wavy margins or a few coarse teeth with small hairs especially on the margins.

Although in the same family as the tomato and potato, all parts of this plant are highly **poisonous**.

Apr–Nov ● Ma, So, Na, Me

to 90 cm, 3 ft

Small-flowered Nightshade

Yerba Buena

Satureja douglasii
Mint Family, *Lamiaceae*

This fragrant perennial favors shady woods near the coast and coast ranges. Short stems arise from above ground woody branches that creep along and root in the soil. Leaves are opposite, and oval to nearly round, with blunt toothed margins and resin filled dots on the surface. White to lavender tiny, single flowers grow on individual stems. They are tubular with two short lips at the mouth. A combination of creeping stems, blunt toothed leaf margins, and single flowers distinguish this plant from other members of the Mint Family.

Yerba Buena makes a superb tea, which may be why it is called "good herb."

This is a lovely, strongly fragrant, spreading ground cover. It likes shade to part shade and moisture in the garden.

Apr–Sep ● Ma, So, Na, Me
3–30 cm, 1–12 in

Yerba Buena

California Skullcap

California Skullcap

Scutellaria californica
Mint Family,
Lamiaceae

The short blooming season makes this shy, somewhat low growing plant easy to miss. A little known native perennial ground cover, it spreads gracefully with many small white snapdragon like flowers. Flowers are white to pale yellow and sometimes tinged pink or blue, tubular, and found in pairs at each pair of opposite leaves. The leaves are linear to oblong. Occasionally found in gravelly habitats.

This is a good plant for dry, light shade in the garden.

Jun–Jul ● Ma, So, Na, Me
15–40 cm, 6–15 in

Alumroot

Heuchera micrantha
Saxifrage Family, *Saxifragaceae*

In deep canyons, on shaded rocky slopes, and moist banks of rocks is where you may discover this common perennial. The small, dainty white flower parts are in fives on waving, erect stems with maple like leaves. Frequently, the leaves are reddish veined.

Heuchera pilosissima is similar, but more compact and densely hairy, and grows on coastal bluffs.

Medicinally, the leaves of Alumroot are often used as a very potent astringent, hence the common name.

In the garden, Alumroot is a favorite for shade and somewhat drier soil.

May–Jul ● Ma, So, Na, Me
15–75 cm, 6–30 in

Alumroot

Woodland Star

Lithophragma affine
Saxifrage Family, *Saxifragaceae*

This delicate perennial is commonly found on moist shady slopes or rocky meadows where its small dainty white petals and round leaves are welcome sights in early spring. On thin stems the five petals are mostly three toothed and appear to be stars floating above the grasses. The leaves are rounded and lobed forming small rosettes. Sometimes the leaves become reddish or purple.

A very similar plant is Hillside Star, *Lithophragma heterophyllum*, with flower petals that are not toothed. Also, to tell these plants apart, look at the flower base where it is V shaped in Woodland Star and U shaped in Hillside Star.

Useful as well as pretty, Woodland Star was valued by Native Americans who chewed the roots for colds and stomach aches.

A highly sought after ornamental, Woodland Star loves shade and is tolerant of water. They are best when massed and go well with such companions as Clarkias, Shooting Stars, and Fairy Lanters. Give them a place near the front of the garden so their beauty won't be missed.

Mar–May ● Ma, So, Na, Me
15–60 cm, 6–24 in

California Saxifrage
Saxifraga californica
Saxifrage Family, *Saxifragaceae*

Just before spring bids farewell to winter, be on the lookout for this low grow-ing perennial with its five dainty white petals and red stamens. The leaf-less flower stem is above a basal rosette of oblong shaped leaves that are fuzzy with small teeth. Common to moist, shady banks, the California Saxi-frage is finished blooming by early summer.

In a garden setting they are vulnerable to snails and slugs.

Feb–Jun ● Ma, So, Na, Me
10–30 cm, 4–12 in

Wood Saxifrage
Saxifraga mertensiana
Saxifrage Family,
Saxifragaceae

In late winter as you hike along streams and damp rocky areas, the dainty white flowers and round leaves of this native perennial cannot easily be overlooked. But as more showy plants appear in the late spring and summer, these low growing tiny blooms may be easy to miss. Found only in the two more northern and coastal of our four counties, the Wood Saxifrage is a charming find at any time.

Feb–Jul ● So, Me
15–30 cm, 6–12 in

Wood Saxifrage

Sugarscoop
Tiarella trifoliata var. *unifoliata*
Saxifrage Family, *Saxifragaceae*

Sometimes called Foam Flower, Sugarscoop is occasionally seen in shady places along stream banks, and in moist woods. An early to mid summer bloomer, the tiny white flowers have many hair like stamens protruding

beyond the five petals. A slender hairy stem has slightly toothed, heart shaped leaves, with larger leaves near the bottom. The seed capsules look like miniature old fashioned sugar scoops, hence the common name.

Native Americans used the roots to make a tea to treat diarrhea in children and chewed fresh leaves as a cough medicine.

May–Jul ●
Ma, So, Me
10–50 cm, 4–20 in

Sugarscoop

Beach Strawberry
Fragaria chiloensis
Rose Family, *Rosaceae*

This low spreading perennial is commonly found on coastal bluffs and moist sand dunes. The white flowers have five pointed petals with many stamens producing edible red berries that are fairly tasteless. The leaves are wedge shaped, shiny, dark green with lateral veins, finely toothed, and densely hairy on the underside.

Beach Strawberry is one of the two parents of most, if not all, cultivated strawberries. *Fragaria virginiana* is the other parent.

This plant is a good ground cover with sun and irrigation.

Mar–Aug ● Ma, So, Me
5–20 cm, 2–8 in

Beach Strawberry

Woodland Strawberry
Fragaria vesca
Rose Family, *Rosaceae*

This low growing perennial is common to shady, open woods. The flower has five white petals and many stamens and produces a smaller fruit than the typical garden strawberry. The elliptical leaves are lightly to densely hairy with green leaf stalks and flower stems sometimes lightly tinged with reddish purple.

The edible berries are pleasingly flavored and commercially cultivated in

small quantities for the gourmet market. Herbal tea made from the leaves, stems, and flowers is believed to aid in the treatment of diarrhea.

In the garden this plant provides good ground cover especially in shady locations. It will spread by stolons and the offsets are easily transplanted.

Mar–Jun ● Ma, So, Na, Me
3–30 cm, 1–12 in

Woodland Strawberry ●

Ocean Bluff Milkvetch

Ocean Bluff Milkvetch

Astragalus nuttallii
var. *virgatus*
Pea Family, *Fabaceae*

Endemic to California and found only in our coastal counties, this low growing plant is not often seen. When it is, the unusual seed pod of this perennial suits its occasional reference as "Rattleweed." The puffed pods look like tiny rattles as the seeds ripen. From 20-125 cream colored flowers nod on their stem. The leaves are formed of 21-43 fuzzy oblong leaflets. This very short plant is subdued in color, from the muted cream of the flowers to the dusty gray green of the foliage.

Apr–Jul ● Ma, So, Me
3–10 cm, 1–4 in

Salt Marsh Dodder

Cuscuta salina
Dodder Family,
Cuscutaceae

Salt Marsh Dodder is a parasitic plant occurring in coastal salt marshes. Despite the delicate white tubular flowers its wiry, twining, orange stems envelop Alkali Heath, Jaumea, Pickleweed, and other salt marsh plants. It appears that masses of spaghetti have been dropped on its host. Having no roots and almost no chlorophyll, their leaves are reduced to tiny scales.

Other local Dodders are typically yellow in color and are found in many habitats, both moist and dry.

May–Sep ● Ma, So, Na, Me
Twines on host

Salt Marsh Dodder

Coast Manroot

Marah oreganus
Gourd Family, *Cucurbitaceae*

Coast Manroot

These little white, male, bell shaped flowers can be found in canyons and hilly areas. The long vine produces a 5-8 cm, 2-3 in, melon shaped fruit with tiny weak spines. The large, broad leaves with 5-7 shallow but sharp pointed lobes, green fruit, and corkscrew tendrils are easily visible as the plant crawls across occasional boulders.

A very similar plant is California Manroot with cream colored, flat star shaped flowers. The fruit has rigid spines.

California Indians pounded the massive root for toxins to use in streams and tide pools to stun fish. The root was also used for soap.

Can be difficult to establish in the garden, but is there to stay once it is. If planting for the fruit be certain to have a female plant.

Mar–May ● Ma, So, Na, Me
Vine 1–6 m, 3–20 ft

Modesty

Whipplea modesta
Mock-orange Family, *Philadelphaceae*

Modesty

A common, appealing little subshrub usually found in open or shady places on dry or rocky slopes, banks or in forests. It has trailing, slightly woody stems and somewhat inconspicuous flowers. Five or six white spreading petals form flowers that crowd into terminal clusters. The small white buds look like tiny snowballs that suddenly open to reveal a most interesting flower. Leaves are egg shaped to elliptical, and generally deciduous; in coastal areas they are evergreen.

This is an excellent low growing ground cover for shady places. It favors good soil, good drainage, some shade and will take regular garden water.

Apr–Jun ● Ma, So, Na, Me
5–15 cm, 2–6 in

Philadelphia Fleabane

Erigeron philadelphicus
Sunflower Family, *Asteraceae*

Each little flower head has hundreds of fine ray flowers surrounding the center of yellow disk flowers. The basal leaves on this perennial herb are oblong to lance shaped. It is found in moist, open grassy habitat and is found throughout the United States and Canada.

The name Fleabane refers to its believed properties to repel fleas. Tannins in Fleabane protect cuts from infections and promote skin tissue healing.

Don't confuse this plant with the invasive *E. karvinskianus* which should not be planted.

Apr–Jul ● Ma, So, Na, Me
25–80 cm, 10–30 in

Coltsfoot

Petasites frigidus var. *palmatus*
Sunflower Family, *Asteraceae*

The large, palm shaped leaves are basal and look nothing like a colt's foot. The cluster of terminal blooms are purplish pink or white and there seems to be no equestrian reference here either. However, more fitting is *Petasites* meaning "hat with a broad brim," alluding to the leaves. This native plant of moist stream banks and seep areas blooms in early spring.

Mar–Apr ● Ma, So, Na, Me
20–60 cm, 8–24 in

Coltsfoot

Trail Plant

Adenocaulon bicolor
Sunflower Family, *Asteraceae*

In the shaded forests of the North Coast Ranges the miniature white 1-5 flowered heads of the native Trail Plant may be seen. One must look closely, as it is very tiny and well camouflaged on its long, thin stem. It is the leaves at the base of the stem which give this plant its name and are easily spotted. When the dark green, triangular leaves are disturbed or turned over the whitish under leaf is displayed. One could follow the trail of another passing through the woods or mark your own trail.

Jun–Aug ● Ma, So, Na, Me
30–90 cm, 1–3 ft

Trail Plant

Common Yarrow

Common Yarrow
Achillea millefolium
Sunflower Family,
Asteraceae

A fragrant bloom is atop a stem covered with tiny white cottony hairs. The flat topped clusters are comprised of 3-6 white to pink ray flowers. The delicate fern like leaves, thousand leaved *millefolium* or finely divided, are flat and lacy green on this native perennial.

Common Yarrow has many medicinal claims.

Plant in sun/part shade for native gardens. Not particularly invasive, easy to control and care for.

Mar–Nov ● Ma, So, Na, Me
30–90 cm, 1–3 ft

Brownie Thistle
Cirsium quercetorum
Sunflower Family, *Asteraceae*

One can just imagine a brownie or elfin character gathering with other miniscule creatures around the deeply lobed, spikey leaves of this low growing native thistle. The cream, yellow or brown colored blooms may be seen in summer on the coastal bluffs.

May–Jul ● Ma, So, Na, Me
10–15 cm, 4–6 in

Brownie Thistle

Yellow

Seep-spring Monkey Flower

Mimulus guttatus
Broom-rape Family, *Orobanchaceae*

This highly variable plant is commonly found in wet places along the banks of creeks and streams, and seeps in banks or bluffs. You may also find it in open areas from sea level to the mountains. The plant can be short or tall, thin and spindly, or large and bushy. The yellow flowers have five petals united into a tube with two lips. There are often reddish spots near the opening of the tube with a hairy hump nearly closing the tube at the base. Stems are erect with the leaves egg shaped to round.

This plant and other *Mimulus* were recently moved from the Figwort Family, *Scrophulariaceae*.

Seep-spring Monkey Flower favors sunny locations in the garden and goes well in a water garden or containers.

Mar–Aug ● Ma, So, Na, Me
3–150 cm, 1–60 in

Cream Sacs

Cream Sacs

Castilleja rubicundula
ssp. *lithospermoides*
Broom-rape Family,
Orobanchaceae

Common to all four of our counties,
these bright yellow annual flowers of
five petals united in two lipped tubes
remind one of tiny sacs of butter
cream, as the common name implies.
Found widely in spring through early
summer, the butter yellow blossoms
with lance shaped and thread like
lobed green bracts are common to
grassy, open areas.

Recently moved from the Figwort
Family, *Scrophulariaceae*.

Apr–Jun ● Ma, So, Na, Me
20–75 cm, 8–30 in

Butter and Eggs

Triphysaria eriantha ssp. *eriantha*
Broom-rape Family, *Orobanchaceae*

The yellow color of this small spring wildflower is how it earned its vivid
common name. This plant has flowers of five petals united in a two lipped
tubular flower and three yellow sacs. A red purple hooked beak is above the
sacs. The showy color of
the flowers is nicely offset
by the purple of the up-
per leaves and bracts. You
will find fields of these
cheerful little treasures in
the grass lands of all four
of our counties.

Recently moved from
the Figwort Family,
Scrophulariaceae.

Mar–May ● Ma, So, Na, Me
5–35 cm, 2–14 in

Butter and Eggs

Musk Monkey Flower
Mimulus moschatus
Broom-rape Family, *Orobanchaceae*

This prostrate, late summer flower is commonly found in wet soil near streams or creeks in all four of our counties. It may also occur in dry riverbeds. The

yellow flower has five petals united into a tube with two lips formed of two and three lobes. Lower petals have red streaks in the center and on the two ridges in the throat. Oblong leaves are covered with long, soft hairs.

Recently moved from the Figwort Family, *Scrophulariaceae*.

A good low growing perennial that works well in water gardens or containers.

Jun–Aug ● Ma, So, Na, Me
5–30 cm, 2–12 in

Musk Monkey Flower

Yellow Sand Verbena
Abronia latifolia
Four O'Clock Family, *Nyctaginaceae*

Like most coastal natives, these fleshy leafed plants favor beach conditions—sun and sand. Locally common to our coastal dunes and scrub, this long blooming perennial sometimes grows in large, dense, green mats of foliage sporting many golden yellow balls of flowers. Each round flower ball sitting atop its short, erect, sturdy stem is formed of numerous small, trumpet shaped flowers.

Native Americans sometimes ate the stout roots of this plant.

May–Oct ● Ma, So, Me
Prostrate

Yellow Sand Verbena

Golden Fairy Lantern
Calochortus amabilis
Lily Family, *Liliaceae*

Small yellow flowers nodding gracefully as though a tiny fairy's lantern give this perennial its enchanting common name. Found in chaparral, foothill woodlands, and mixed evergreen forests, the blossoms are bright yellow, sometimes yellow orange. Preferring shade they are often found peeking out from under a shrub. Three

petals form the spherical, drooping flower which is closed at the tip. Three yellow sepals spread horizontally above the flower. Leaves are basal and the foliage is generally covered with a light powdery film that rubs off easily.

Available from specialty nurseries, do NOT dig in the wild.

Apr–Jun ● Ma, So, Na, Me
10–45 cm, 4–18 in

Golden Fairy Lantern

Gold Nuggets
Calochortus luteus
Lily Family, *Liliaceae*

A bright yellow California native occurring in grasslands, foothill woodlands, and mixed evergreen forests. The sunshine yellow, bell shaped flower is formed of three open, wedge shaped petals. Each petal has a red brown central blotch with numerous red brown freckles nearby with short little hairs near the base of the petal. The leaves are less impressive, linear and basal and

certainly upstaged by this spectacular, showy flower.

For the garden note that the bulbs are sold as *C. luteus* var. Golden Orb.

Apr–Jun ● Ma, So, Na, Me
20–45 cm, 8–18 in

Gold Nuggets

Tiburon Mariposa Lily

Calochortus tiburonensis
Lily Family, *Liliaceae*

This very rare native can only be found in a single serpentine outcrop in Marin County, Ring Mountain Preserve. Three large triangular petals form the exotic looking greenish yellow flower. Each petal is detailed with a thin dark circular line and the inner surface is covered with long pale hairs. Three sepals, fused at the tips, stick out like thorns between the petals. Long, thin, pointed green leaves turn to bronze and curl under; the underside is dull green.

This plant is threatened by loss of habitat due to recreational activities and competition from invasive species. The land where this plant survives is in a preserved area.

June ● Ma
30–60 cm, 1–2 ft

Tiburon Mariposa Lily

Fernald's Iris

Fernald's Iris

Iris fernaldii
Iris Family, *Iridaceae*

This perennial rhizome favors the dappled shade and rich humus soil of inland woodlands. The yellow, cream or white flower has a yellow spot and pale yellow veins. Six petals form a long funnel shaped floral tube with three petals up and three down. Stems and the base of the linear leaves are a reddish brown wine color. The tube above the ovary is very long and funnel like near the top.

Similar to Purdy's Iris, but these flowers do not have an open spread to their sepals and petals.

April–May ● Ma, So, Na, Me
15–45 cm, 6–18 in

Purdy's Iris

Iris purdyi
Iris Family, *Iridaceae*

This low growing, endemic rhizome with its large flower with spreading petals and sepals thrives in open habitats. The six pale cream yellow, or whitish with purple tinge, petals have prominent reddish brown or purple veins. They form a long funnel shaped, floral tube. As the flower matures the petals and sepals spread open and flatten somewhat. Short, overlapping bract like leaves enclose the stem. Plants grow as individuals or in sparse clumps.

Similar to Fernald's Iris, this plant is the only Pacific Coast Iris that has a truncate stigma, a pistil broad at the end. The white spreading flower has a very unique look.

> **May–Jun ● Ma, So, Na, Me**
> **5–30 cm, 2–12 in**

Purdy's Iris

Yellow-eyed Grass

Sisyrinchium californicum
Iris Family, *Iridaceae*

This perennial produces a profusion of charming little yellow flowers in wet habitats along the coast in late spring. The flowers are short lived but the plant produces many buds which continue to bloom through spring and summer. Six oblong, slightly concave petals form a small upright floral tube. The petals are spread out equally from the center of the flower. The leaves are dark green and grass like.

The pretty spring flowers and foliage make this a great smaller perennial for garden borders. Each bloom provides a bright and sunny spot in the garden. Loves moist sites and wetlands. Spreads easily, though not aggressively.

> **May–Jun ● Ma, So, Na, Me**
> **15–60 cm, 6–24 in**

Yellow-eyed Grass

American Winter Cress
Barbarea orthoceras
Mustard Family, *Brassicaceae*

In moist places along streams and in meadows, the terminal cluster of yellow flowers with four petals appears in early spring. By August, long seed pods appear on the native American Winter Cress. The upper leaves of this perennial are pinnate while the basal leaves are large and have a terminal rounded lobe. The stem is succulent like.

May–Sep ● Ma, So, Na, Me
20–40 cm, 8–15 in

Western Wallflower

Erysimum capitatum
Mustard Family, *Brassicaceae*

A pretty yellow or orange, four petaled, typical mustard bloom appears atop a tall stout stem with linear leaves. This native perennial is a delightful sight in many dry and rocky locations in the coastal woodlands.

Western Wallflower is highly variable with many subspecies.

Mar–Jul ● Ma, So, Na, Me
15–90 cm, 6–36 in

Western Wallflower

San Francisco Wallflower

Erysimum franciscanum
Mustard Family, *Brassicaceae*

The rounded, four petaled maltese cross like bloom of this perennial are cream, aging to dark yellow. Leaves of this rare, endemic dune dweller are linear and toothed. At the end of summer erect seed pods may be seen forming on the stem beneath the top blooms.

Similar to *Erysimum menziesii* ssp. *concinnum* an endangered species more likely to be found on fresh dunes and coastal headlands. With a bloom time of Mar-May it may be found in our three coastal counties.

Mar–Jun ● Ma, So
5–45 cm, 2–15 in

San Francisco Wallflower

Beach Evening Primrose
Camissonia cheiranthifolia
Evening Primrose Family, *Onagraceae*

This beach baby is a common coastal plant found on sand dunes and beaches. It favors full sun and sand. First forming a rosette of whitish gray foliage, the plant produces prostrate shoots that grow in many directions. The spread-

ing foliage sometimes forms large, dense mats. The solitary flowers are yellow, turning to reddish. They are formed from four bright yellow petals, sometimes with one or two red spots near the base. Short lived, each flower opens at dawn and blooms for only one day.

**Apr–Aug ● Ma, So, Na, Me
Prostrate stems 60 cm, 2 ft**

Beach Evening Primrose

Sun Cup
Camissonia ovata
Evening Primrose Family,
Onagraceae

A harbinger of spring, this very charming plant has great smile appeal. The bright yellow cup like flower is nestled in a circle of equally bright green leaves. Four petals form the flower and all flower parts are vivid sunshine yellow. There is no stem, as what looks like a stem is really a very long flower tube, and the ovary is hidden underground. Common to grassy areas.

In the garden they'll take some foot traffic and grow happily in the toughest clay soil.

**Mar–Jun ● Ma, So, Na, Me
Ground hugger**

Sun Cup

Hooker's Evening Primrose

Oenothera elata ssp. *hookeri*
Evening Primrose Family, *Onagraceae*

This tall, showy native pleasures summer evening strollers along moist coastal and slightly inland bluffs. Also found along coastal marsh edges, its pretty and quite fragrant flowers bloom in late afternoon and at dusk. Sometimes quite tall, this plant has hairy, lance shaped leaves. Clusters of bright yellow, fading to reddish orange flowers, with four heart shaped petals are borne atop leafy long stems.

This is a showy biennial with beautiful yellow flowers that appear the second year. It reseeds profusely in the garden, needs low to moderate water, good drainage, and does well in sandy soils. Common in wildflower seed mixes.

Jun–Sep ● Ma, So, Na, Me
30–150 cm, 1–5 ft

Hooker's Evening Primrose

California Buttercup

Ranunculus californicus
Buttercup Family, *Ranunculaceae*

This cheerful yellow charmer is a welcome sight in late winter. One of the most common of our wildflowers, its Latin name means "little frog" for its preference for wet meadows, damp slopes and generally moist habitats.

The plant has waxy flowers of 7-22 white to lemon yellow petals forming a little cup. Petals have a shiny upper surface and a nectar gland at the base of each. The wedge shaped leaves are toothed or deeply cut and feathery on the ends.

Native Americans boiled the roots, roasted the seeds and extracted yellow dye from the flowers.

Feb–May ● Ma, So, Na, Me
15–60 cm, 6–24 in

California Buttercup

Western Buttercup
Ranunculus occidentalis
Buttercup Family, *Ranunculaceae*

This showy, sunny wildflower carpets moist grassy meadows or open wood-lands in the full sun of early spring. The plant has a branching stem with single, bright yellow flowers at the end of each branch. Each flower has 5-6 glossy yellow petals surrounding a center of yellow stamens and pistils. The three lobed basal leaves are close to the ground while smaller leaves are attached directly to the flowering branches. The leaves are either smooth or softly hairy.

Western Buttercup is similar to California Buttercup and Bloomer's Buttercup.

> **Mar–May ● Ma, So, Na, Me**
> **10–60 cm, 4–24 in**

Western Buttercup

Bloomer's Buttercup
Ranunculus orthorhynchus var. *bloomeri*
Buttercup Family, *Ranunculaceae*

Bright yellow buttercups are always a welcome sight in the early days of spring. This somewhat uncommon and relatively low grower makes its home in wet meadows and on bluff tops. Easily confused with both the Western Buttercup and the California Buttercup, the five glossy yellow petals of this plant are larger than both by comparison, and the leaves are varied on reddish, slightly hairy stems. The stem helps to differentiate Bloomer's Buttercup.

> **Mar–May ● Ma, So, Na, Me**
> **15–45 cm, 6–18 in**

Bloomer's Buttercup

Meadow Rue
Thalictrum fendleri var. *polycarpum*
Buttercup Family, *Ranunculaceae*

A plant with elegant foliage and unusual flowers, Meadow Rue is common to moist, shady slopes near streams and meadows. Any one plant has all male or all female flowers. The numerous pendulous, yellow green flowers have no petals which may make them seem less attractive. But tassel like stamens give this flower special eye appeal. As stamens fade brown, they contrast with the white sepals to give the flowers a festive look. The leaves are compound.

Meadow Rue is attractive to bees, butterflies and birds.

Mar–Jun ● Ma, So, Na, Me
30–91 cm, 1–3 ft

Meadow Rue

Yellow Pond Lily
Nuphar luteum ssp. *polysepalum*
Water Lily Family, *Nymphaeaceae*

Solitary golden flowers on dark floating leaves make this perennial the most beautiful aquatic plant in our region. Usually seen at a distance, the plants rise from thick underground rhizomes anchored to the bottom of a pond or slow moving stream. Large thick and waxy heart shaped leaves 10-40 cm, 4-16 in, long float on the water attached to stems that can grow to six feet in length. Bright yellow flowers tinged with red are formed of 10-20 petals, many stamens, and a stigmatic disk in the center.

Native Americans used the rootstocks and seeds as a source of food.

Apr–Sep ● Ma, So, Na, Me
Aquatic

Yellow Pond Lily

Tinker's Penny
Hypericum anagalloides
St. John's Wort Family, *Hypericaceae*

Thick mats of bright green, tangled looking leaves grow in moist meadows and along small drainages. The plant stems creep flat against the ground. El-liptical leaves arise and roots descend from this mat at each node of the stem, producing a clone of the parent plant. At the tip of each upturned leaf stem knobby buds give way to small, golden yellow flowers. They are formed by five petals and five sepals. Stamens that are sometimes black dotted, dance gently with each breeze.

Jun–Aug ● Ma, So, Na, Me
Prostrate

Tinker's Penny

Goldwire
Hypericum concinnum
St. John's Wort Family, *Hypericaceae*

The yellow flowers of this low growing plant dance in the summer breezes on the dry, brushy slopes of our four counties. Slender wiry stems bear 3-9 flowers and linear to lance like leaves that are generally folded upward and

sparsely freckled with tiny black dots. Five oblong narrow petals form a proud golden yellow flower that puffs out its chest of many golden stamens sporting golden anthers. The look is very wiry, very gold.

The Klamath Weed is similar but an invasive weed and taller plant.

May–Jul ● Ma, So, Na, Me
10–40 cm, 4–16 in

Goldwire

Blazing Star

Mentzelia laevicaulis
Loasa Family, *Loasaceae*

One of the showiest flowers in our region is found on this perennial native to sandy to rocky slopes, washes and road cuts. The large yellow flower commands full attention. When fully open it is 10-15 cm, 4-6 in, wide with five bright yellow petals and a wide fountain like display of numerous long stamens. Gray triangular leaves with bristly, toothed margins are borne on tall, erect stems.

A showy plant that does well in a sunny, well drained spot with minimal water.

Jun–Oct ● Ma, So, Na, Me
30–90 cm, 1–3 ft

Blazing Star

Pine Violet

Viola lobata
Viola Family, *Violaceae*

The Pine Violet is a charming little wildflower with five, vivid yellow petals which may have purple veins. Found on dry, open or wooded slopes. This low growing perennial has broad, dark green, moose horn lobed foliage that nicely offsets the bright yellow flowers.

Apr–Jul ● So, Na, Me
5–45 cm, 2–18 in

Pine Violet

Johnny Jump-up
Viola pedunculata
Viola Family, *Violaceae*

A late winter, early spring bloomer, Johnny Jump-up can be found on open grassy slopes and in oak woodlands. The plant is often low growing, but can also reach more than a foot in height. The flowers are yellow with five large petals, some with dark brown veins.

California natives picked the young, delta shaped leaves in late winter before the flowers appeared and boiled them for food.

This is not the Johnny Jump-up of nursery fame.

Feb–Apr ● Ma, So, Na, Me
5–40 cm, 2–16 in

Johnny Jump-up

Redwood Violet
Viola sempervirens
Viola Family, *Violaceae*

Preferring cool, mostly shady woods, this low growing perennial is a late winter, early spring bloomer. Also called Evergreen Violet, its dark green delta to kidney shaped foliage does not die back in winter. The bright yellow flowers have five large petals. Four petals point upward and are generally smaller, while the larger fifth petal forms a lower lip that comes to a point at the very

tip. The lower petal and nearest upper petals are detailed with dark veins.

A tea can be made from the dried leaves of this plant.

Feb–Apr ●
Ma, So, Na, Me
1–30 cm, ¹/₂–12 in

Redwood Violet

Canyon Dudleya

Dudleya cymosa
Stonecrop Family, *Crassulaceae*

A loose oval cluster of succulent leaves form the base for a fleshy stalk with smaller, intermittent, thick alternate leaves. The bloom, a yellow to red little urn formed by the five narrow, lance like petals, is apparent atop this native found on hot rocky cliffs.

This species of succulent gets its name from Stanford University botany professor William R. Dudley (1849-1911).

Another common name is Live Forever.

This perennial ground cover would do well in part shade in a rock garden.

Apr–Jun ● Ma, So, Na, Me
10–20 cm, 4–8 in

Canyon Dudleya

Powdery Dudleya

Dudleya farinosa
Stonecrop Family, *Crassulaceae*

This coastal succulent can be seen growing on craggy, weathered, sandstone monoliths. Pale lemon yellow blooms have urn like petals, similar to Canyon Dudleya. With elliptical light blue green, basal leaves it looks like an eccentric artist's conception on the gray rock outcrops that are covered with lime green and bright rust red lichens.

Powdery Dudleya is a perennial ground cover that likes part shade and works well in a rock garden. Intolerant of drought in sandy soils.

May–Sep ● Ma, So, Me
10–35 cm, 4–14 in

Powdery Dudleya

Pacific Sedum

Sedum spathulifolium
Stonecrop Family, *Crassulaceae*

Pacific Sedum is a perennial with a flat basal rosette of leaves and the flower stem arising from the center. This center stem differentiates *Sedums* from *Dudleyas* where it comes from the side. Small yellow flowers have five petals and are star like. It is found blooming in open rocky coastal locations.

A good succulent ground cover that likes part shade and works well in a rock garden.

May–Jul ● Ma, So, Na, Me
5–20 cm, 2–12 in

Pacific Sedum

California Lomatium

Lomatium californicum
Carrot Family, *Apiaceae*

The cream to yellow umbel flower of this perennial may be found on open slopes, brushy woodlands, forest and chaparral. Five tiny petals form the flower above delicate blue grey foliage.

The young tender stalks of these large leafed plants were eaten by California Indians. The roots were chewed and smoked.

Although not common in cultivation, California Lomatium can be used in well drained soil in shade to part sun. It is a host plant for the Anise Swallowtail butterfly.

Apr–Jun ● Ma, So, Na, Me
30–120 cm, 12–48 in

California Lomatium

Footsteps of Spring

Sanicula arctopoides
Carrot Family, *Apiaceae*

Coastal headlands are covered with this lovely low growing mat of yellow button like blooms. The mats are extensive and seeds with spiny hooks have caused casual coastal hikers to do a herky jerky barefoot dance as a reaction to careless foot placement. The leaf is yellow green and three parted, forming a rosette.

Difficult in gardens, not commonly cultivated.

Feb–May ● Ma, So, Me
5–20 cm, 2–8 in

Footsteps of Spring ○

Coast Sanicle

Sanicula laciniata
Carrot Family, *Apiaceae*

The delicate yellow flowers of this *Sanicula* are atop short, stout stems. Leaves are deeply divided with margins sharply angled and toothed. It is quite common and found in many coastal habitats from open or brushy slopes to mixed evergreen woodlands.

Difficult in gardens, not commonly cultivated.

Feb–Apr ●
Ma, So, Na, Me
5–30 cm, 2–12 in

Coast Sanicle

Sticky Cinquefoil

Potentilla glandulosa
Rose Family, *Rosaceae*

A common plant of many habitats with smallish cream colored to pale yellow petals that are mostly in clusters. This perennial has upper stems with glandular hairs that may feel somewhat sticky, hence the common name. The leaves are reminiscent of strawberry, strongly toothed, but with more leaflets.

An easy to grow plant for the garden with flowers lasting longer with part shade and moderate water.

May–Jul ●
Ma, So, Na, Me
to 80 cm, 32 in

Sticky Cinquefoil

Silverweed

Potentilla anserina ssp. *pacifica*
Rose Family, *Rosaceae*

Coastal brackish marshes, moist meadows, and stream banks along the Pacific Coast from Alaska to Southern California are home to this common, creeping, perennial herb. Its tufted, feather like leaves of 7-31 leaflets are silver below. Plants form large patches that are connected to each other by runners. A single yellow, five petaled flower with many stamens sits atop a leafless, sometimes slightly hairy stalk.

Silverweed was grown for food and medicine in the past. The cooked root is said to taste like sweet potato.

Apr–Aug ● Ma, So, Na, Me
3–75 cm, 1–30 in

Silverweed

Deerweed
Lotus scoparius
Pea Family, *Fabaceae*

From spring through summer this shrubby plant is covered in small yellow flowers that attract bees and butterflies. Commonly found in chaparral, coastal sand, and roadsides, the flowers grow in clusters of 1-7 flowers. The bright yellow petals are pea shaped clusters that turn red as they age. Stems are green, erect and somewhat branched with small compound leaves of 3-6 leaflets. It resembles a miniature dreaded Scotch Broom, but this is a friendly native.

This plant thrives after fires, helps reduce erosion, and enriches soil with nitrogen with the help of symbiotic bacteria.

A great bushy perennial that likes full sun and low water. Good for stabilizing slopes.

Mar–Aug ● Ma, So, Na, Me
15–60 cm, 6–24 in

Deerweed

False Lupine

Thermopsis macrophylla
Pea Family, *Fabaceae*

This grayish, fuzzy leafed perennial is frequently spotted in meadows, grasslands and forest openings, and is common to serpentine outcroppings, and chaparral. Bright yellow lupine like flowers appear for a short, late spring blooming season. Petals form pea shaped clusters borne on erect stems. Leaves are lance shaped and compound with three leaflets.

This native resembles lupines, hence its common name.

May–Jun ● Ma, So, Na, Me
61–120 cm, 2–4 ft

False Lupine

Narrow-leaved Mule Ears

Wyethia angustifolia
Sunflower Family, *Asteraceae*

The playful name evokes images of beasts of burden used in this area before mechanization. Captain Wyeth (1802-1856) who discovered this many petalled yellow perennial, was probably quite familiar with mules. The leaf is long, linear and tapering. You will find this native plant on open grassy hillsides.

California Indians used the seeds of this shade loving plant in pinole mixtures and ate the raw green narrow leaves.

Similar plants are the other Mule Ears with the leaves being clues to their identity.

Apr–Jul ● Ma, So, Na, Me
30–90 cm, 1–3 ft

Narrow-leaved Mule Ears

Coast Mule Ears

Wyethia glabra
Sunflower Family,
Asteraceae

The large, dark green, oblong to oval leaves of the native Coast Mule Ears distinguish it from its narrow leafed relative. Also, it may be found in open dry places. This perennial has many petalled yellow blooms.

As are all the various Mule Ears, Nathaniel Wyeth's name is a part of this genus. He is best known in botany for his discovery of the Mule Ears.

Seeds of all the Mule Ears were used in pinole by California Indians.

Mar–May ● Ma, So, Na, Me
10–40 cm, 4–16 in

Coast Mule Ears

Gray Mule Ears

Wyethia helenioides
Sunflower Family, *Asteraceae*

The tiny gray hairs on the large leafed Gray Mule Ears distinguish it from its relatives. This native perennial has a similar yellow, many petalled bloom but appears less frequently and may be found in forest meadows.

Nathaniel Wyeth, for whom this plant is named, was one of the great pioneers of Oregon.

Mar–Jul ● So, Na, Me
30–75 cm, 12–30 in

Gray Mule Ears

California Helianthella

California Helianthella

Helianthella californica
Sunflower Family,
Asteraceae

The native California Helianthella is found in open spaces along the coastal slopes. Its sunflower style yellow blooms are visible from April through June. The reddish stem may reach 60 cm, 2 ft, tall and the leaves of this perennial herb are linear to broad, rounded apex with a tapering base.

Apr–Jun ● Ma, So, Na, Me
15–60 cm, 6–24 in

Blow Wives
Achyrachaena mollis
Sunflower Family, *Asteraceae*

Blow Wives seedhead

This little native sunflower of grasslands and foothill woodlands has an almost unnoticeable yellow to red bloom in spring. Ray and disk flowers are barely above the erect green bracts of the head. The flower heads are yellow and honeycomb like. When in seed, pappus form a shiny white round head. As the name suggests, seed dispersal is achieved by the blowing wind. The leaf is simple, entire.

Apr–May ● Ma, So, Na, Me
2.55–40 cm, 1–15 in

Nodding Harmonia
Harmonia nutans
Sunflower Family, *Asteraceae*

The elusive little rare, yellow Nodding Harmonia is an annual herb that appears in rocky soils, openings in chaparral or woodlands, and volcanic substrates. It is very similar to Goldfields which grows in masses in the same environment. Look for the notched petals to draw your attention to its identity.

Also known as *Madia nutans*.

Its seeds may have been used in pinole mixes of coastal California Indians.

Apr–June ● So, Na
5–25 cm, 2–10 in

Nodding Harmonia

Common Hareleaf
Lagophylla ramosissima
Sunflower Family, *Asteraceae*

This slender, branched annual herb may grow to 120 cm, 4 ft, tall with gray green, linear leaves covered in fine hairs. The small yellow rayed flower heads open in late afternoon and close the following midmorning. Found in dry open areas in the coastal hills.

May–Oct ● Ma, So, Na, Me
15–120 cm, 6–48 in

Common Hareleaf

Hayfield Tarweed
Hemizonia congesta
Sunflower Family, *Asteraceae*

If ever an aroma matched a common name, then this annual herb of coastal grasslands and fallow fields is a prime example. When the linear to narrowly elliptical leaves of this native are crushed underfoot or between one's fingers, a pleasant, distinctive odor of tar is produced. The little yellow or white, 5-13 rayed petals appear in early summer through October.

June–Oct ●
Ma, So, Na, Me
10–80 cm, 4–32 in

Hayfield Tarweed

Fitch's Spikeweed

Centromadia fitchii
Sunflower Family, *Asteraceae*

The stiff, spiny tips of this native tarweed may prick you when encountered. Perhaps Reverend Fitch (1794-1874) may have been hiking on the open coastal slopes and before smelling the strong, pungent odor of this little yellow rayed flower, may have felt its presence. Each flower head of this annual herb has 10-20 light yellow ray flowers.

Formerly named *Hemizonia fitchii*.

May–Nov ● Ma, So, Na, Me
10–50 cm, 4–20 in

Fitch's Spikeweed

Common Madia

Madia elegans
Sunflower Family, *Asteraceae*

In grassland and open forest this strongly scented native Common Madia may be found. Like its other *Madia* relatives the flowers have yellow disk like blooms. Often you may find a maroon blotch at the base of the deeply lobed rays. There are soft hairy to bristly, linear to lance shaped leaves with a strong resinous odor.

With fifteen species or subspecies of *Madia* in our four counties, they can sometimes be quite challenging to properly identify.

The seeds, or fruits, are nutritious and were used by California Indians in preparing pinole.

May–Sep ●
Ma, So, Na, Me
15–75 cm,
6–30 in

Common Madia

Jaumea
Jaumea carnosa
Sunflower Family, *Asteraceae*

The Spanish "con carne" meaning "with meat" may serve to
indicate that *Jaumea carnosa* has
meaty stems which often weigh
down the plant into a prostrate
position. The foot long stems of
this perennial herb are topped
with a small thickly composited
yellow rayed sunflower. The
low, ground hugging Jaumea are
found in coastal salt marshes.

May–Oct ● Ma, So, Na, Me
10–30 cm, 4–12 in

Jaumea

Coastal Sneezeweed
Helenium bolanderi
Sunflower Family, *Asteraceae*

This perennial of coastal bluffs and moist meadows blooms from June through
August. The large, toothed ray flowers surround the purple brown head of
disk flowers. The leaves are lance like, toothless, and extend down the stem.

Leaves were once
dried and powdered
for snuff, hence the
name Sneezeweed.

Jun–Aug ● So, Me
30–60 cm, 1–2 ft

Sneezeweed

Coastal Tidy Tips

Layia platyglossa
Sunflower Family, *Asteraceae*

A more delicate descriptive name may not be found in titles of coastal wild-flowers than that of Coastal Tidy Tips. The 5-18 little yellow ray flowers in each bloom are white tipped. Leaves of this native plant are linear with margins smooth or possible short lobes. These beauties decorate many open grassy areas and coastal bluffs. This perennial herb personifies a classic coastal wildflower.

Seed is readily available and easy to grow if protected from slugs and snails.

May–Jun ● Ma, So, Na, Me
10–30 cm, 4–12 in

Woolly Sunflower

Eriophyllum lanatum var. *arachnoideum*
Sunflower Family, *Asteraceae*

The yellow 8-13 rayed bloom of the perennial Woolly Sunflower may be found in open, dry locations along the coast and in the hills. Clumps of the branched hairy leafless stems are very common from April to August. The foliage is grayish and woolly.

In the garden this native enjoys part shade.

Apr–Aug ● Ma, So, Na, Me
15–90 cm, 6–36 in

Woolly Sunflower

Goldfields

Lasthenia californica
Sunflower Family, *Asteraceae*

Most coastal residents and visitors will be struck by the extensive blankets of gold covering many coastal bluffs and open fields from March to May. Upon closer inspection the covering is constructed of thousands of tiny yellow rayed flowers. Also found on inland hills, the leaves of this native plant are linear to broad rounded apex and tapering base.

Mar–May ● Ma, So, Na, Me
to 40 cm, 16 in

Goldfields

Goldfields
flow across the land
bonding together
to make up for small size

Common Blennosperma

Blennosperma nanum
Sunflower Family, *Asteraceae*

This annual, which often grows in masses, is closely related to the daisy. The oval flower head bracts are a pale yellow with purple on the back. The ring of stamens emits a viscous white juice containing the pollen. The seeds are also carried in a sticky gooey fluid. The name "blenna" comes from the Greek meaning "slimy seed." Lower leaves are 7-15 lobed on succulent stems. It is common as masses in wetlands, valley grasslands, foothill woodlands and is often a resident of vernal pool floral communities.

Feb–Apr ● Ma, So, Na, Me
5–20 cm, 2–8 in

Common Blennosperma

Sonoma Sunshine

Blennosperma bakeri
Sunflower Family, *Asteraceae*

Closely related and very similar in appearance to Common Blennosperma, Sonoma Sunshine is a much more pleasing descriptor than its generic cousin's moniker. An endangered species, its bracts are yellow and the lower leaf lobes are entire or three lobed. The lobes are longer than those of Common Blennosperma. You may find this annual herb in vernal pools and wet grasslands.

Feb–Apr ● So
5–20 cm, 2–8 in

Sonoma Sunshine

Lizard Tail

Eriophyllum staechadifolium
Sunflower Family, *Asteraceae*

Found on maritime headlands in sunny spots where one may find a lizard, this woolly sunflower is a small shrubby plant normally in a mounded cluster. The name Lizard Tail may come from the short, deeply toothed leaves that are soft and woolly, covered with tiny white hairs underneath. The lovely smoky green foliage is decorated with many clusters of yellow daisy like flowers.

California Indians dried and ground the seeds into flour.

A cast iron plant useful for coastal erosion control or planting on harsh slopes.

May–Nov ● Ma, So, Na, Me
to 60 cm, 2 ft

Lizard Tail

California Butterweed

Senecio aronicoides
Sunflower Family, *Asteraceae*

In forest openings and coastal oak woodlands, the little clusters of yellow pincushion blooms of this native perennial can be found. Leaves are oblong to egg shaped, wavy or shallowly toothed in a basal circle. The nearly leafless stem yields a milky sap when broken, however please don't feel the need to test this.

Apr–Jul ● Ma, So, Na, Me
30–90 cm, 1–3 ft

California Butterweed

Cape Ivy

Senecio mikanioides
Sunflower Family, *Asteraceae*

This malicious, alien invader of many coastal riparian areas can be seen climbing on living plants and trees and covering rocks and topsoil. Its yellow flowers bloom in winter as many non native species do because of their transplantation from a different eco zone. The shiny green five pointed leaves are characteristically odorous, in other words they stink!

Cape Ivy can easily spread by resprouting from small pieces of the plant making it difficult to successfully remove. Cape Ivy kills native plants by enveloping them in a heavy blanket of vegetation which blocks out the light.

Cal-IPC ranks it A for impact and invasiveness.

Also known as Germany Ivy and *Delairea odorata*.

Dec–Feb ● Ma, So, Na, Me
Climbing vine

Pearly Everlasting

Anaphalis margaritacea
Sunflower Family, *Asteraceae*

Blooming throughout the summer the oval flower heads of white papery bracts surround yellow disk flowers. The thin long linear leaves are alternately arranged along the stem of this common aromatic perennial herb. This native is found in foothill woodlands, chaparral, valley grasslands, and forests.

Jun–Aug ● Ma, So, Na, Me
15–90 cm, 6–36 in

Pearly Everlasting

Purple Everlasting

Gnaphalium purpureum
Sunflower Family,
Asteraceae

Purple Everlasting is an unscented annual or biennial herb growing on dry, often disturbed or waste places. The tiny brown or purplish flowers on this native species are in dense spike like clusters atop a stalk with occasional oblong to lance shaped, leaves. Sometimes the leaves are purplish. *Gnaphalium* is Greek for "lock of wool," certainly fitting for this woolly little plant.

Also known as *Gamochaeta purpurea*.

Apr–Jul ● Ma, So, Na, Me
5–60 cm, 2–24 in

Purple Everlasting

Yellow Star Thistle

Centaurea solstitialis
Sunflower Family, *Asteraceae*

The prickly bane of over 12 million acres of California landscape, the Yellow Star Thistle is an invasive, persistent pest. The bloom consists of long yellow spines extending menacingly from the yellow flower heads. The stout, ridged, cottony stem has nondescript linear leaves. This invasive non native annual weed blooms in disturbed places, grasslands and woodlands.

The Yellow Star Thistle plant has the ability to create monotypic stands in fields that prevent other species from growing there. Whole fields of solid Yellow Star Thistle are not uncommon. Its competitiveness and lack of natural enemies make it a very successful invader. The plant is a pest in field crops, prevents domestic animals' grazing in rangelands, acts as a physical barrier to wild animal movement in wildlands, and is toxic to horses. Cal-IPC rates this plant "A" in impact and distribution, and "B" in invasiveness.

May–Oct ● Ma, So, Na, Me
30–150 cm, 1–5 ft

Gumplant

Grindelia stricta var. *platyphylla*
Sunflower Family, *Asteraceae*

A little yellow sunflower, this native Gumplant is found on windswept coastal bluffs and dunes. The immature "bud" found atop the stem contains a distinct white gummy liquid. It appears above oblong, tongue like leaves.

Gumplant blooms throughout the summer making it a good low growing perennial herb with low to moderate water needs in the garden.

The gummy substance was used as a topical skin lotion by California Indians.

May–Sep ● Ma, So, Me
10–20 cm, 4–8 in

California Mugwort

Artemisia douglasiana
Sunflower Family, *Asteraceae*

The cute and cryptic common name Mugwort may conjure up strange images, the herb has been given dream inducing attributes through time.

Growing to 2.5 m, 8 ft, under good conditions in open to shady locations such as foothill woodlands, chaparral, and valley grasslands. This perennial has insignificant yellow green blooms arranged with 6-10 ray flowers in a disk.

California Mugwort has fragrant foliage which was used by California Indians to relieve the effects of Poison Oak. Chumash used it to discourage insects in stored acorns.

Good for stabilizing or restoring disturbed areas with moderate summer water. For the residential garden this native is best in a container as it is highly invasive.

Jun–Dec ● Ma, So, Na, Me
.5–2.5 m, 1¹/₂–8 ft

California Mugwort

California Goldenrod

Solidago californica
Sunflower Family,
Asteraceae

Just the sound of the name makes some want to sneeze, but the tall stem of this native is said to be a healer of wounds. This common perennial's tall, stout stem has numerous yellow rayed flower heads atop it in a spike like terminal cluster. The leaf is broad oblong to elliptical. You can find California Goldenrod in forest openings, clearings and fields.

Jul–Oct ● Ma, So, Na, Me
30–120 cm, 1–4 ft

California Goldenrod

California Dandelion
Agoseris grandiflora
Sunflower Family,
Asteraceae

This common native with its many rayed yellow to red flowers, blooms in various coastal environments from May through July. The multi lobed basal leaves form a rosette. You will find this perennial herb in foothill woodlands, chaparral, valley grasslands, and woodlands.

May–Jul ● Ma, So, Na, Me
6–12 cm, 2–5 in

California Dandelion

Yellow Skunk Cabbage
Lysichiton americanum
Arum Family, *Araceae*

Very large oval leaves, perhaps 1-5 feet wide, accompany the large yellow envelope like bract that surrounds the narrow pokerlike spike of tiny flowers. The flowers are indistinct, yellow green and ill smelling, hence the common name. Found in shady, swampy areas, or stream areas, this plant is uncommon in our area.

Apr–Jul ● Ma, So, Me
30–60 cm, 1–2 ft

Skunk Cabbage

Orange

California Poppy

Eschscholzia californica
Poppy Family, *Papaveraceae*

Perhaps the best known and most celebrated wildflower of the west is the California Poppy. In 1903 the California Poppy was voted our official State flower. This long blooming, free branching poppy with its lacy, bluish green leaves and spectacular flower, brings color and verve to grassy open areas across the state. You may be lucky enough to see a meadow or hillside covered with California Poppies. The bright showy flowers vary from pale yellow to deep orange to bronze, or occasionally rose colors and may have double or semi double blossoms. Four shiny petals form a bowl shaped, long lasting flower, which closes at night and opens again when the sun appears. Named for J. F. Eschscholtz (note the spelling) naturalist on Russian expeditions in California during 1816. A similar plant is Tufted Poppy, *Eschscholzia caespitosa*, which is smaller with longer stamens giving it a tufted look. It is found in open chaparral areas.

The poppy was cherished by California Indians both as a source of food and for the oil extracted.

The plant reseeds well and favors dry sunny locations. It is a colorful addition to your garden.

Feb–Sep ● Ma, So, Na, Me
5–60 cm, 2–24 in

Wind Poppy

Stylomecon heterophylla
Poppy Family, *Papaveraceae*

This wonderful native annual with its orange red flowers is occasionally found on grassy and brushy slopes, and openings in chaparral. Four showy wedge shaped petals with a dark brown blotch at the base form solitary flowers on erect little stems. In the center of the flower are many free stamens. The upper leaves are compound while the lower basal leaves are simple and wider with toothed or notched margins.

For a good color spot in the native garden plant this charming flower in sun to broken shade. It reseeds nicely and will return each year with little effort.

Apr–May ● Ma, So, Na
30–60 cm, 1–2 ft

Wind Poppy

Common Fiddleneck

Amsinckia menziesii var. *intermedia*
Forget-me-not Family, *Boraginaceae*

Tiny orange trumpet flowers appear along the upper edge of a coil that suggests the head of a violin. Named for Archibald Menzies who appears throughout botanical literature. The fiddleneck seems an appropriate namesake for him as a fellow Scot, John Lowe, composed a fiddle tune in the naturalist's honor, "Archie Menzies Reel" in 1840. Menzies was the surgeon and naturalist who explored the Pacific Northwest with George Vancouver in the 1790's.

The seeds and leaves of Common Fiddleneck may be toxic to livestock.

Amsinckia intermedia was the former name of this plant.

Mar–Jun ● Ma, So, Na, Me
15–90 cm, 6–36 in

Common Fiddleneck

Large-flowered Collomia

Collomia grandiflora
Phlox Family, *Polemoniaceae*

A showy native occasionally found in open areas. Five petals form trumpet like flowers in a cluster typical of the phloxes, so there is no surprise here.

What is remarkable are the apricot to butterscotch colored flowers that can be seen in the small buds of the image above. Also, typical of the phlox family are their blue pollen tipped anthers. The flower head is atop a sturdy stem with lance to linear leaves.

In good soil with average water this plant will become quite tall. In poor conditions, it stays closer to the ground

Apr–Jul ● Ma, So, Na, Me
15–90 cm, 6–36 in

Scarlet Fritillary
Fritillaria recurva
Lily Family, *Liliaceae*

This very charming, smooth, gray green plant is found on dry hillsides, woods or brush in three of our counties. Narrow, pale gray leaves climb the flower stalk with most leaves near the middle of the stem. Leaves are linear in 1-3 whorls. Hanging in an open raceme at the top are 1-5 nodding, narrow bell shaped, orange to red flowers with yellow spotting inside. The petals are recurved.

A choice specimen for the edge of a woodland garden. A colony of this showiest of the Fritillaries is a beautiful sight. Purchase from a reliable source.

Mar–Jun ● So, Na, Me
30–90 cm, 1–3 ft

Scarlet Fritillary

Leopard Lily
Lilium pardalinum
Lily Family, *Liliaceae*

This very tall member of the Lily family has orange flowers with maroon spots earning its common name. Each stem bears from 1-35 pendant flowers. The six petals are strongly reflexed displaying long stamens and the pistil in a very showy manner. Occasionally found in moist places and stream banks. Elliptical leaves grace the stems in 1-8 whorls; margins are not wavy.

Lilium pardalinum ssp. *pitkinense* and *pardalinum* are very similar to the Leopard Lily. All three are endemic to California.

May–Jul ● Ma, So, Na, Me
to 3 m, 10 ft

Leopard Lily

Coast Lily

Coast Lily

Coast Lily
Lilium maritimum
Lily Family, *Liliaceae*

This rare, endemic species with its short blooming season is only occasionally found in bog like areas in sandy, wet meadows, forest, and scrub within a few miles of the ocean. Stems bear 1-13 chubby nodding flowers that are held horizontally. Each is formed of six red orange petals and is spotted purple in its golden throat. The floral tube is reflexed at the lip displaying six colorful

stamens. Leaves are scattered along the stem or in whorls; margins are not wavy.

Lilies are known to hybridize and there are various forms of the Coast Lily.

Jun–Jul ● Ma, So, Me
to 2 m, 7 ft

Coast Lily

Pitkin Marsh Lily
Lilium pardalinum ssp. *pitkinense*
Lily Family, *Liliaceae*

Primarily pollinated by hummingbirds, this endemic, perennial bulb grows in marshes and oak scrub. Most lilies grow among other vegetation which supports their height.

Only three populations of this endangered species have ever been discovered. Collection of plants, seeds, and bulbs, loss of habitat, and competition from invasive species are rapidly depleting plant numbers of this and other endangered species.

Lilium pardalinum ssp. *pardalinum* and ssp. *pitkinense* are barely distinct from one another.

Jun–Jul ● So
to 3 m, 10 ft

Pitkin Marsh Lily

Spotted Coralroot
Corallorrhiza maculata
Orchid Family, *Orchidaceae*

Both Mertens' Coralroot and Striped Coralroot are similar to Spotted Coralroot. All are found in shady conifer forests, all have red brown to yellow

brown leaves sheathing the stem, and all have the typical sepals and petals forming a lipped orchid flower. But the colors and markings can help distinguish between them. Spotted Coral Root is orange, reddish or yellow with a white three lobed lip with crimson spots. The stem is orange yellow.

The above name is recognized as current, but there is a spelling variant of *Corallorhiza maculata*.

Jun–Aug ● Ma, So, Na, Me
15–76 cm, 6–30 in

Spotted Coralroot

Striped Coralroot

Corallorrhiza striata
Orchid Family, *Orchidaceae*

Occasionally found in rich wooded areas, this plant has few discernible leaves that clasp tightly to the red to brown stem. Depending on fungi of the forest floor for nutrients, this shameless perennial demands attention with its flashy striped spike and waxy flowers. The flower spike is clustered with sometimes 15-25 orange white orchid like flowers with red stripes. Each flower has an arching petal that forms a little hood, four lateral petals and a tongue shaped lip. Similar to Mertens' Coralroot and Spotted Coralroot, the red stripes on the petals help to distinguish this plant from the others.

May–Jul ● Ma, So, Na, Me
15–60 cm, 6–24 in

Striped Coralroot

Mertens' Coralroot

Corallorrhiza mertensiana
Orchid Family, *Orchidaceae*

Found in shady conifer forests, but only in our two most northern counties, this plant has nearly indiscernible red brown to yellow brown leaves sheathing the stem. Dark orange, reddish, or yellow sepals and petals form the typical lipped flower of the Orchid Family. The white lip petal has dark red lines that help to distinguish this from other Coralroots, but the prominent spur immediately behind the petals locks the identification as Mertens' Coralroot.

Jun–Jul ● So, Me
15–46 cm, 6–18 in

Mertens' Coralroot

Stream Orchid

Epipactis gigantea
Orchid Family, *Orchidaceae*

This attractive member of the Orchid Family may be spotted along stream banks, in wet meadows and seeps. The small flowers with their rich but subtle colors are pale yellow brown to yellow green with purple veins. Look closely, they are quite elegant against their large leaves. Three petal like sepals and two petals form a typical orchid flower. The orange lip is strongly marked with red lines. Large, lance shaped leaves with strongly parallel veins clasp the stem.

The Stream Orchid shown here is the purplish black leaved form from The Cedars, a serpentine area in western Sonoma County.

Other common local names are Stream Orchis and Chatter Box Orchid. The flowers are hinged and when moved by a breeze appear to be chattering.

May–Aug ● Ma, So, Na, Me
30–76 cm, 12–30 in

Stream Orchid

Leopard Lilies
stalk spring
looking for a word
to rhyme with orange

Pink to
Red

Cardinal Monkey Flower

Mimulus cardinalis
Broom-rape Family, *Orobanchaceae*

Found commonly in moist areas along creeks and banks of streams. This long blooming flower is a colorful contrast to its dark green foliage. The five orange to red petals of the flower are united into the two lipped tube typical of *Mimulus*.

Juice of the plant can be used to soothe minor burns.

This plant has been recently moved from the Figwort Family, *Scrophulariaceae*. Also known as Scarlet Monkey Flower.

Cardinal Monkey Flower will thrive in sunny locations with good water in the garden. Very good lower growing perennial with nice bright flowers.

Apr–Oct ● Ma, So, Na, Me
30–75 cm, 1–3 ft

Cardinal Monkey Flower

Kellogg's Monkey Flower

Mimulus kelloggii
Broom-rape Family, *Orobanchaceae*

These eye catching little beauties in their bright pink to purple bonnets are welcome cheery annuals on damp disturbed soil. This small plant typically grows in dense mats, but also in small groups between rocks and gravel.

Petals shade from deep red at the base to deep pink or purple at the tip, giving the flowers an intense red purple color. They form a floral tube with a deep, dark interior. Two large upper lobes with three smaller lower lobes give this flower their sun bonnet appearance. The stamens are bright yellow in contrast to the floral tube. This charming flower is a gem to enjoy in the spring.

This plant has been recently moved from the Figwort Family, *Scrophulariaceae*.

Mar–Jun ● So, Na, Me
1–30 cm, ¹/₂–12 in

Kellogg's Monkey Flower

Pink Butter and Eggs
Triphysaria eriantha ssp. *rosea*
Broom-rape Family, *Orobanchaceae*

This small spring wildflower is a rose dusted version of the yellow and orange colors found in the flowers of Butter and Eggs. A lovely low, prolific plant sporting blooms with five petals united in two lipped tubular flowers. You will find blankets of these cheerful little beauties flowing across the grassy fields of coastal hills.

This plant has been recently moved from the Figwort Family, *Scrophulariaceae.*

**Mar–May ● Ma, So, Na, Me
10–35 cm, 4–14 in**

Pink Butter and Eggs

Pt. Reyes Birds Beak
Cordylanthus maritimus
ssp. *palustris*
Broom-rape Family,
Orobanchaceae

Blooming from late spring through early fall, you might think it easy to find this rare plant; that is not the case. Locally it is found only in the salt marshes of Marin and Sonoma Counties with its largest populations in Humboldt County and Oregon. Its pale flowers do not grab the attention of more showy blooms. If you are lucky enough to find this flower, be sure to take a photo and enjoy this treasure, as you may not see one again.

This plant has been recently moved from the Figwort Family, *Scrophulariaceae.*

**May–Oct ● Ma, So
10–40 cm, 4–15 in**

Pt. Reyes Birds Beak

Sticky Chinese Houses

Collinsia tinctoria
Figwort Family, *Scrophulariaceae*

Although not as rare as Round Headed Chinese Houses of sand dunes, nor as common as Purple Chinese Houses of shady areas, Sticky Chinese Houses are occasionally found in the stony areas of three of our counties. The pale yellow to lavender flowers are typical of *Collinsia* with five petals united into a two lipped tube. Like the other Chinese Houses, the characteristic that distinguishes this plant is the ring of flowers around the stem which make them look like Chinese pagodas.

May–Aug ● So, Na, Me
20–60 cm, 8–24 in

Purple Owl's Clover

Castilleja exserta
Broom-rape Family, *Orobanchaceae*

After a wet spring, acres of grassy slopes, fields and open areas are commonly carpeted with this beautiful flower. Not very tall, this lovely little annual plant has linear, lobed leaves and small pouched flowers peeking out from colorful yellow to rose or white to purplish red bracts. The flowers have five petals united as a two lipped tube, with two lobes up and three lobes down.

Medicinally, the plants have been used for "women's diseases," rheumatism, and as an astringent.

This plant has been recently moved from the Figwort Family, *Scrophulariaceae*.

Mar–May ● Ma, So, Na, Me
10–45 cm, 4–18 in

Indian Warrior...
stout American native
found in small bands
friendly

Indian Warrior
Pedicularis densiflora
Broom-rape Family, *Orobanchaceae*

This very early perennial has a long blooming season that begins in winter and extends into early summer. The five petals of its vivid red flower are united into a two lipped tube. The compound leaves complement the flowers of this low growing perennial. Before the flower blooms one may confuse the leaves for that of a fern. Common to dry brushy slopes, the Indian Warrior is an early harbinger of the flowers of spring. In good years you may be lucky to see bands of Indian Warriors beneath the trees.

This plant has been recently moved from the Figwort Family, *Scrophulariaceae*.

Jan–Jun ● Ma, So, Na, Me
8–50 cm, 3–20 in

Wight's Paintbrush
Castilleja wightii
Broom-rape Family, *Orobanchaceae*

This coastal paintbrush has a long blooming season so is commonly enjoyed
throughout spring and summer. As with
other *Castilleja*, the red to yellow flower
leaf bracts have five petals united into a
two lipped tube which are nicely set off by
the foliage. The lower leaves are linear and
the upper leaves have three sharp pointed
lobes. You will not find this plant far from
the coast.

This plant has been recently moved from
the Figwort Family, *Scrophulariaceae*.

Mar–Jul ● Ma, So, Me
30–90 cm, 1–3 ft

Wight's Paintbrush

Paintbrush
Castilleja spp.
Broom-rape Family,
Orobanchaceae

It's easy to see how the *Castilleja* gets its common name Paintbrush. A cluster of straight
stems with showy flower bracts at the top
resemble a paintbrush just dipped in
paint. Known for its bright reds, the colors
actually vary from orange to scarlet to
purple, even yellow or white. It is the
flower leaf bracts surrounding the actual
flower, which may sometimes be almost
hidden, that give the plant its vivid color.
Leaves vary, but may be long, narrow, and
pointed, without teeth with fine hairs on
the upper leaves.

Growing in varied habitats, this plant is a
favorite food for the larvae of butterfly species.

This genus has been recently moved from
the Figwort Family, *Scrophulariaceae*.

Mar–Sept ● Ma, So, Na, Me
to 60 cm, 2 ft

Paintbrush

California Indian Pink...
God bored
with lobed petals
took his shears
gave these an edge

California Indian Pink

Silene californica
Pink Family, *Caryophyllaceae*

This native Pink is almost brick red in color and a charming sight decorating chaparral and open woodlands. Its genus name, *Silene*, is derived from the Greek name for a forest spirit often associated with Dionysus the god of wine. The five, bright red, four lobed petals of this perennial herb are on top of a light green stem with opposite, linear, lance like leaves. Certainly the most showy *Silene*.

Mar–Aug ● Ma, So, Na, Me
15–30 cm, 5–12 in

Lemmon's Catchfly

Silene lemmonii
Pink Family,
Caryophyllaceae

The native perennial with its pink-ish, nodding, five petalled, tubular flowers is found in oak wood-lands, coastal hills and coniferous forests. As its name suggests, the tiny sticky hairs sometimes catch small insects. The long leaf is oblong. A delicate little dancer to come upon in the woods.

Jun–Aug ● Ma, So, Na, Me
15–40 cm, 5–15 in

Lemmon's Catchfly

Henderson's Shooting Star

Dodecatheon hendersonii
Primrose Family, *Primulaceae*

This perky little charmer is found in shady serpentine, grassland, and open ar-eas in the woodlands. An early harbinger of spring, it stands out for its swept back petals and forward pointed, pollen bearing stamens. Four to five petals in pink, lavender, or white have a dark purple band at their base and a yellow band edged with white just above that. The green leaves are elliptical to egg shaped. Their basal rosettes dry up in summer and begin their cycle of growth with fall and winter rains.

Roasted leaves and roots were eaten by California Indians.

Gardeners often plant Shooting Stars in meadows and on banks to enjoy its beautiful, interesting blos-soms.

Feb–May ● Ma, So, Na, Me
30–60 cm, 1–2 ft

Henderson's Shooting Star

Shooting Stars
blaze across winter's
dark ground
heralding spring
granting the wish
for new things

False Baby Stars

Linanthus androsaceus
Phlox Family, *Polemoniaceae*

In mid to late spring a profusion of perky pink flowers in open or shaded areas in woodlands and chaparral are most likely this pretty annual. An erect little plant that is not very tall and its leaves are scarce, but the flowers command attention. Pink to lilac to white phlox like flowers occur in dense, terminal heads. Each flower is a small upright trumpet of five colorful petals with the throat of the trumpet generally violet at the base and yellow above. The leaves are divided into linear segments, sometimes prickly and clustered near the top.

False Baby Stars

These are lovely garden flowers to seed in sunny, dry locations.

Apr–Jun ● Ma, So, Na, Me
5–30 cm, 2–12 in

True Baby Stars

Linanthus bicolor
Phlox Family, *Polemoniaceae*

The very charming name does justice to this fragrant, pleasant annual. Common to open, grassy areas, chaparral, and woodlands, this low growing plant with its pink or white flowers is a welcome sight in spring. The petals of the small flowers form a non flaring tube with a bright yellow throat that is ringed with white. The tube has five lobes which stand out stiffly at right angles to the base. Flowers stand erect on very long slender stems that emerge from

a star like cluster of linear leaves. This long stem is a differentiation between False and True Baby Stars, very similar plants.

Mar–Jun ● Ma, So, Na, Me
3–16 cm, 1–6 in

True Baby Stars

*Pussy Ears delicately
tuned to the flutter of
bird and butterfly wings and
the skitter scatter of dormice*

Pussy Ears

Calochortus tolmiei
Lily Family, *Liliaceae*

The unusual flower of this low grow-
ing perennial makes it easy to identify. At home in
varied habitats the three white pink to purplish petals
that form this flower are densely hairy inside. The flowers do indeed look like the ears of sleeping kittens. The
leaves are linear, basal and longer than the flower stalk.
They will be the first sign of this plant, looking like a
long feeler to gauge the weather. This is a charming
flower to discover.

Apr–Jun ● Ma, So, Na, Me
10–40 cm, 4–15 in

Andrew's Clintonia

Clintonia andrewsiana
Lily Family,
Liliaceae

The showy pink to rose purple flowers of this coastal redwood forest perennial are very attractive. Six petals form a small floral cup that clusters with others in an umbel on a tall stem. The four or five leaves are elliptical, shiny, and basal. There are few hairs along the leaf margin. Later in the season the fruit berries add another splash of color. They are bright blue and bead like containing small black seeds, hence, another common name of Blue Bead.

May–Jul ● Ma, So, Me
15–60 cm, ¹/₂ –2 ft

Western Trillium

Western Trillium

Trillium ovatum
Lily Family, *Liliaceae*

This native perennial is sometimes called Wake Robin because it appears when the robins return from winter migration. It is common to moist, wooded or brushy habitats. Like all Trillium, parts of the plant come in groups of threes. The open flower is formed by three white petals and three sepals, and rises above three large leaves on a short stem. The leaves are net veined and form a whorl on a naked green stem. The white flower petals change to pink as they age. Western Trillium is easy to distinguish from other Trilliums because it is the only species that has a stem between the flower and the leaves.

Feb–Apr ● Ma, So, Na, Me
15–75 cm, 6–30 in

Common Trillium

Trillium chloropetalum
Lily Family, *Liliaceae*

A single erect flower rises directly from the center of the large leaves in spring. The color of the flower varies from white to yellow to purple and is wonderfully offset by purple stamens and the bright or dark green foliage. Trillium refers to the flower parts in threes. Three very large, broad, purple mottled leaves form a single whorl with three petals form-ing the flower which sits tightly against the leaves.

This native is similar to Sweet Trillium.

Feb–Jul ● Ma, So, Na, Me
20–75 cm, 8–30 in

Common Trillium

Trillium (in threes)
netted veined leaves
sepal and petal
delighting to stream's
splash and ripple
pure blossoms gleaming

Sweet Trillium

Trillium albidum
Lily Family, *Liliaceae*

If you come across a damp shade plant that reminds you of a very expensive appetizer offered in an equally pricey restaurant, you have likely found this unusual perennial. Three broad leaves in a single whorl most elegantly offer this white to pink flower for your viewing pleasure. Three petals form the flower which sits tightly against the leaves. The leaves are oval and brown spotted. Trillium refers to the flower parts in threes. This native is similar to Common Trillium.

Trilliums are good in a shade garden or in containers. Don't be tempted to pick the flowers as the plant will not survive. Please don't dig plants in the wild, but rather purchase them from reputable nurseries.

Apr–May ● Ma, So, Na, Me
20–75 cm, 8–30 in

Cascade Onion

Allium cratericola
Lily Family, *Liliaceae*

Cratericola means one who dwells at the mouth of volcanoes. Favoring chaparral, open serpentine and especially volcanic areas, this endemic perennial has earned its name. A wild onion, large colonies of Cascade Onion may be found by the odor of onion in the air. The leaves are shiny, green and linear with a thick green midrib on the outside, but the flower is the eye catcher. Dense clusters of attractive pink flowers against sparse, neat foliage give this plant particular appeal. Six petals form the flower. Although small in stature, this plant makes a large floral statement.

Mar–Jun ● Na, Me
3–10 cm, 1–4 in

Cascade Onion

One-leaf Onion

Allium unifolium
Lily Family, *Liliaceae*

If you spot tiny, pink or white star shaped flowers blooming in dense umbels on damp, sometimes clay soil in late spring to early summer you have likely found this delightful perennial. Six petals form each tiny flower standing on a short erect stem attached to the main flower stalk. Two to three keeled, linear leaves offset the blossoms. A distinct onion odor will be present.

This plant is uncommon in the wild, but is fast becoming a common garden addition. It is ideal for mass plantings and borders; wildlife resistant; and increases rapidly. Check your nursery or the Resource section for a supplier. Do not dig in the wild.

Apr–Jun ● Ma, So, Na, Me
30–75 cm, 12–30 in

One-leaf Onion

Wild Onion

Allium dichlamydeum
Lily Family, *Liliaceae*

If sea cliff breezes have the scent of onions, look for clumps of short, grass like plants on the dry clay soil. If there are clusters of deep red purple flowers in umbels on a thick flower stalk, and it's late spring or summer, there is little doubt as to what you've found. But just to be sure, lightly press the thick stem and sniff for the smell of onion. Six small, pointed petals form each little flower making Wild Onion lovely to look at, but less delightful to smell.

May–Jul ● Ma, So, Me
10–30 cm, 4 to 12 in

Wild Onion

Calypso Orchid

Calypso bulbosa
Orchid Family, *Orchidaceae*

Calypso was a nymph goddess whose captivating beauty delayed Odysseus on his return from Troy in Homer's *Odyssey*. This exceptional, captivating, low growing orchid is a perfect namesake. Often difficult to spot, the plant is slender, has only a single basal leaf and flower. The bright pink orchid like flower on a tall, thin stem has three sepals and two petals. The sepals are split, and spread wing like from above the hood. The slipper like lip petal is tipped with two horns and mottled with orange, yellow and white. A very attractive orchid of our conifer forests.

Jan–May ● Ma, So, Na, Me
8–25 cm, 3–10 in

Calypso Orchid

Socrates Mine Jewelflower

Socrates Mine Jewelflower

Streptanthus brachiatus
Mustard Family,
Brassicaceae

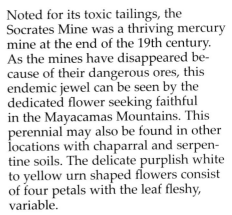

Noted for its toxic tailings, the Socrates Mine was a thriving mercury mine at the end of the 19th century. As the mines have disappeared because of their dangerous ores, this endemic jewel can be seen by the dedicated flower seeking faithful in the Mayacamas Mountains. This perennial may also be found in other locations with chaparral and serpentine soils. The delicate purplish white to yellow urn shaped flowers consist of four petals with the leaf fleshy, variable.

May–Jul ● So, Na
20–60 cm, 8–24 in

Bristly Jewelflower

Streptanthus glandulosus

ssp. *secundus*
Mustard Family,
Brassicaceae

This pretty pink annual blooms atop a stem with linear upper leaves and lower leaves linear with compound lobes. The native Bristly Jewelflower with its four small petals forming urn shaped flowers may be found blooming in rocky soils.

Mar–May ● Ma, So, Me
10–20 cm, 4–8 in

Bristly Jewelflower

Mountain Jewelflower

Streptanthus tortuosus
Mustard Family,
Brassicaceae

Not looking tortured at all as its scientific name suggests, the native Mountain Jewelflower is a delicate pretty little plant. Yellow four petalled urn shaped blooms are surrounded by reddish purple tipped sepals. The heart shaped leaves encircle the stems and are found growing on hot rocky slopes.

Apr–Aug ● Ma, So, Na, Me
15–90 cm, 6–36 in

Mountain Jewelflower

Winecup Clarkia

Clarkia purpurea
Evening Primrose Family, *Onagraceae*

An appealing native often found in open grassland or shrubby habitats where it puts on a show in late spring. Four bowl shaped petals form solitary flowers. They are pink to wine red, often with a red spot in the middle. Flower buds are erect and quite lovely. The hairy leaves are alternate, linear to lance like. Stems are decumbent to erect, reddish green to red and covered with fine hair.

Sometimes included in seed mixes, this plant is a fairly dependable grower from seed.

Apr–Jul ● Ma, So, Na, Me
15–60 cm, 6–24 in

Winecup Clarkia

Red Ribbons
Clarkia concinna
Evening Primrose Family,
Onagraceae

This pretty little annual is commonly seen on grassy or brushy embankments and coastal scrub. It has remarkable flowers that resemble thin red ribbons, hence the common name. The buds of the flowers are covered by long thin sepals. The dark red pink sepals split and separate as the petals expand. Four bright pink petals form the flower. Each petal has three deep, narrow lobes with a white streak running from the center lobe to the base of the petal. Leaves are broadly

oval. Another common name is Lovely Clarkia, but I was told that it's not fair to use that name as all *Clarkias* are lovely!

Plant this interesting native at the front of a garden border or in containers.

May–Jul ● Ma, So, Na, Me
25–30 cm, 10–12 in

Red Ribbons

Elegant Clarkia
Clarkia unguiculata
Evening Primrose Family, *Onagraceae*

This native annual can be found along trails and roads in woodlands, on open slopes, chaparral, and valley grasslands. It is easy to recognize from the distinctive windmill shape of its showy flowers. Each flower has four petals shading from dark red at the thread like base to pink or purple on the triangular to round lobe. Four slightly hairy green to red sepals are united and turned to one side. Leaves are linear, alternate, and toothed.

This plant is also known as Clarkia Elegans and is endemic to California.

A long lasting cut flower from your garden, this plant can be easily grown from seed. Do not pick in the wild.

May–Jun ● Ma, So, Na, Me
30–90 cm, 1–3 ft

Elegant Clarkia

Farewell to Spring

Clarkia amoena
Evening Primrose Family, *Onagraceae*

This popular summer flower is commonly found on grassy flats and slopes, and in coastal seaside habitats. Flower buds are erect. They unfurl into pink flowers with a red spot near the middle of the petal, giving it a subtle, water-color like character. The four showy petals are bowl shaped. Leaves are linear to lance shaped.

This is an excellent annual for the garden or containers. It will have the greatest effect planted in drifts. It tolerates seaside conditions. Bees are attracted to the flowers.

Jun–Aug ● Ma, So, Na, Me
to 1 m, 1–3 ft

Watson's Fireweed

Epilobium ciliatum ssp. *watsonii*
Evening Primrose Family, *Onagraceae*

This robust and densely leafy plant is occasionally found near fresh water marshes and in wetland habitats. Its cheery, sturdy looking deep pink to rose purple flowers grow on long, slightly hairy stems. Flowers have four deeply bilobed petals. The leaves are lance shaped and slightly hairy with conspicuous veins.

May–Aug ● Ma, So, Na, Me
30–90 cm, 1–3 ft

Watson's Fireweed

Zauschneria

Epilobium canum
Evening Primrose Family, *Onagraceae*

This late blooming native perennial certainly does attract hummingbirds. Its bright crimson to orange red flowers are thin long tubes with four notched lobes. The dark green to gray green leaves are linear to oval and may have toothed edges. This plant blooms until first frost.

There are many horticultural varieties with one known as California Fuchsia. A moderately low plant, this is a perfect choice for a hot sunny area of the garden. Cut back to the ground in late winter, and pinch back the new growth for a fuller appearance.

Aug–Oct ● Ma, So, Na, Me
10–90 cm, 4–36 in

Zauschneria

Columbine...
heads bowed
shy, embarrassed or
studying?
no one knows

Western Columbine

Aquilegia formosa
Buttercup Family, *Ranunculaceae*

This showy red perennial is commonly found in damp areas, on a north slope in rocky seeps, and sometimes in creeks with water surrounding it. Similar to Serpentine Columbine, the Western Columbine is more common, and has smaller flowers and more delicate looking foliage. The flowers are stout and straight with red spurs, red sepals and five yellow petals. The maple like leaves are green on top and gray green underneath.

Native Americans boiled the greens as a vegetable and enjoyed the flowers like candy, sucking the sweet nectar from the flower spurs.

A good nectar source that will attract hummingbirds, bees, and butterflies, this plant favors shade and water in the garden.

Jun–Aug ● Ma, So, Na, Me
30–120 cm, 1–4 ft

Western Columbine

Serpentine Columbine

Aquilegia eximia
Buttercup Family, *Ranunculaceae*

Despite its long flowering season and rather tall height, this showy perennial with red orange flowers and green gray maple like foliage is not easy to find, yet it is well worth seeking. The flowers are a marvel of natural design. Hanging upside down from a curved stem, the sepals and petals look like five small tubes with oversized covers surrounding the many stamens, like an intricate decoration for a holiday tree. Look for this plant near seepage spots and serpentine areas in partial shade inland, and partial shade or full sun near the coast.

Also known as Van Houtte's Columbine.

In the garden, this plant loves shade and water. Birds, butterflies, and hummingbirds are attracted to this very interesting flower.

May–Aug ● Ma, So, Na, Me
30–150 cm, 1–5 ft

Serpentine Columbine

Canyon Delphinium
Delphinium nudicaule
Buttercup Family, *Ranunculaceae*

A common perennial in our coastal counties, the brilliant red flowers can be a riot of color on dry, sunny slopes and in open woods. Its long spurred, five petaled, tube like flowers sit on wiry stems that are often too weak to hold the flowers erect. The stem base is smooth or hairy and has maple like leaves of three or more lobes.

Native Americans made a tea from the root and used leaves externally to kill skin or hair related parasites.

The plant favors sunny, dry spots in the garden, but watch for slugs and snails which are attracted by its presence.

Mar–Jun ● Ma, So, Na, Me
15–120 cm, 6–48 in

Canyon Delphinium

Redwood Sorrel
Oxalis oregana
Wood Sorrel Family, *Oxalidaceae*

A spreading carpet of three leaf clover type leaves with small pleasant flowers, a preference for shade, and growing throughout a moist conifer forest, you've very likely found this cheerful perennial. However, this is not a clover and can be told from them because the leaves fold up when the sun hits them. Three leaves with two deep lobes and a central vein mirror others in the Wood Sorrel Family. During its long blooming season, five white to deep pink, lightly veined petals form a small upright funnel like flower.

The bright green leaves and light colored flowers make this an attractive ground cover in moist shade. Because it spreads easily, some gardeners use it to suppress weeds.

Apr–Sep ● Ma, So, Me
5–30 cm, 2–12 in

Redwood Sorrel

Bleeding Hearts
hangdog in packs
it's a sad world

Bleeding Heart
Dicentra formosa
Poppy Family, *Papaveraceae*

The blue green foliage of this extremely lovely perennial is a delight in itself, but the dramatic impact of its exotic flowers against the lacy leaves make it even more impressive. Occasionally found in damp, shaded areas, this lovely native blooms from spring into summer with clusters of delicate, nodding flowers. Four petals, two outer and two inner, form rose purple to whitish flowers that dangle over the ferny foliage on erect stems.

An early spring favorite of hummingbirds, this plant is a good ground cover in moist shade gardens with humus soil. It spreads easily and is long blooming making it a true delight.

Mar–Jul ● Ma, So, Na, Me

20–45 cm, 8–18 in

Sticky Sand Spurry

Spergularia macrotheca
Pink Family, *Caryophyllaceae*

This common, hairy, little pink, five petalled perennial herb can be seen blooming in rock outcrops, on coastal bluffs, and marshes in most months. The narrow leaves are triangular and are also covered with tiny hairs making it feel sticky, hence the name Sticky Sand Spurry.

Most of year ● Ma, So, Na, Me
10–50 cm, 4–20 in

Sticky Sand Spurry

Western Peony

Paeonia brownii
Peony Family, *Paeoniaceae*

This shy, native perennial with exotic, showy flowers is found tucked under bushes in open dry pine forests, on dry slopes, and scrubland. Bowl shaped flowers of maroon or bronze with yellow to greenish margins and 5-10 petals droop heavy with many stamens from smooth, slightly branching stems. The steel gray foliage is compound and completely deciduous during drought conditions. The fleshy roots produce new leaves and flowers the following spring.

Medicinally, a tea to treat colds is produced from the roots.

This plant is difficult to grow. It prefers dry shade and should be placed in the garden where it will not receive summer water.

Apr–Jun ● So, Me
15–45 cm, 6–18 in

Western Peony

Seathrift

Armeria maritima ssp. *californica*
Leadwort Family,
Plumbaginaceae

This very appealing perennial provides a welcome splash of color on coastal bluffs and sandy habitats. Five small petals form pink flowers growing in tight round clusters on sturdy, green slightly reddish stems. The leaves are linear, basal, and dense. The bright pink flowers are a beautiful sight against the blue of sea and sky.

This is a lovely plant for garden borders or containers. The foliage is evergreen and the flowers bloom from spring to late summer. Use this plant in coastal gardens where it favors sun and water.

Apr–Aug ● Ma, So, Me
5–50 cm, 2–20 in

Seathrift

Sea Lavender

Limonium californicum
Leadwort Family,
Plumbaginaceae

This native perennial is found occasionally in salt marshes and beaches along the California coast. Its long blooming season and sprays of small pale violet flowers on branching stems make it an attractive find. The five small petals form a pale violet almost white tube with blue lobes. The leaves are wide, wedge to elliptical in shape, and mostly basal. There are no leaves on the flower stems. The image shown here is in bud without flowers blooming.

Several European relatives are cultivated for their flower clusters which are used in dry bouquets.

Jul–Dec ● Ma, So, Na, Me
to 60 cm, 2 ft

Sea Lavender

Fringed Checkerbloom

Sidalcea diploscypha
Mallow Family, *Malvaceae*

Very pretty in delicate pink, this lovely annual is found among mid to late spring flowers on open hillsides and meadows. Five subtly striated pale pink petals form the flower which often has dark pink centers. They generally grow in an open cluster on erect, sometimes decumbent stems. The lower leaves are shallowly lobed while the upper leaves are more deeply lobed and bristly.

Apr–Jun ● Ma, So, Na, Me
40–60 cm, 16–24 in

Checker Mallow
Sidalcea malvaeflora ssp. malvaeflora
Mallow Family, *Malvaceae*

Commonly found on open grassy slopes, this sprawling perennial with hairy stems and distinctive flowers makes this plant easy to identify during its long blooming season. Dense clusters of dark green, bristly, rounded basal leaves with 7-9 shallow lobes surround a tall flower stalk. Pale to deep pink delicate

hollyhock like flowers line the stalk. Prominent white veins on the five petals of each flower give it a lace like, showy appeal. The flowers open in the morning and close at night.

   This is an excellent part decidu-ous ground cover that likes sun to part shade and minimal to moder-ate water.

Mar–Aug ● Ma, So, Na, Me
30–60 cm, 1–2 ft

Checker Mallow

Oregon Checkerbloom
Sidalcea oregana
Mallow Family, *Malvaceae*

You'll find this perennial with its rose pink flowers and deep green foliage in wetland habitats, along the edges of moist meadows and seasonal seeps. Deeply lobed basal leaves produce a tall spike of densely clustered pink to rose colored flowers. Each flower is formed by five oblong petals lightly

streaked with pale pink veins. Typical of the Mallow Family, the filaments of the many stamens are fused into a tube.

   A subspecies, Sonoma County's Kenwood Marsh Checkerbloom, *S. oregana* ssp. *valida*, is on the California en-dangered species list. A larger plant, 90-120 cm, 3-4 ft, and is found only in Sonoma County.

Jun–Jul ● So, Na, Me
20–90 cm, 8–36 in

Oregon Checkerbloom

Bitter Root

Lewisia rediviva
Purslane Family, *Portulacaceae*

Consider yourself lucky when you come across this very low growing perennial. It grows in rocky areas, on loose gravelly slopes, and sometimes serpentine. The flowers are large, 5-8 cm, 1-3 in, across, with 10-19 pink or white petals. The reddish green leaves are linear, low to the ground and nearly hidden when the flower is in bloom. The leaves die back soon after the plant flowers.

In August, 1805, Captain Lewis, of the Lewis and Clark Expedition, first tasted Bitter Root, which he found "naucious to my pallate." On the return trip through Bitterroot Valley, Montana, in July, 1806, he collected a sample. Frederick Pursh (1774-1820) classified the plant and named it for Captain Lewis.

Native Americans used this extremely nutritious root as a diet staple.

**Mar–Jun ● Ma, So, Na,
3–10 cm, 1–4 in**

Redmaids
Calandrinia ciliata
Purslane Family, *Portulacaceae*

This very appealing early spring bloomer dots the fields and open areas of grassy habitats and cultivated fields. The diminutive rose red flowers with their five bright petals are round tipped and showy in spring. The flowers open in the afternoon on sunny days. The leaves are fleshy and linear.

Pretty in a small area of a native garden, this plant can be used to restore disturbed areas as a high proportion of plants will emerge and grow relatively quickly.

Some sources consider Redmaids an alien, however Calflora, our definitive source, considers it native.

Feb–May ● Ma, So, Na, Me
5–60 cm, 2–24 in

Redmaids

Pussy Paws
Calyptridium umbellatum
Purslane Family, *Portulacaceae*

This aptly named native is a rare sight on loose sandy or gravelly areas and only found in our two most northern coastal counties. The white to rose pink clusters of densely packed flowers on prostrate stems really do look like the upturned pads of cats' feet. The flower has four tiny petals with kidney shaped sepals. Red stems radiating from the center of the plant bear dark green spatula like leaves.

May–Aug ● So, Me
5–25 cm, 2–10 in

Pussy Paws

Gypsum Spring Beauty
Claytonia gypsophiloides
Purslane Family, *Portulacaceae*

Good things come in small packages and this little dancer is a case in point. Although short in stature and common to moist, loose soils and serpentine, an up close look at the lovely pink to purple flower reveals yet another uncommon little marvel of nature. Five small petals form the flower with each lightly curved like a shallow ladle and notched at the tip. Each petal has its own thin stamen. Leaves are basal and fused. The look of the flower is open and free like spring itself.

Apr–Jul ● Ma, So, Na, Me
3–25 cm, 1–10 in

Gypsum Spring Beauty

Siberian Candyflower
Claytonia sibirica
Purslane Family, *Portulacaceae*

This charming little perennial is common to moist, densely shaded areas. The flowers bloom through spring and summer, making an attractive carpet in damp places. The flowers are small with five white to pink candy striped petals. The lance to elliptical leaves are shiny and fleshy. The lower leaves are spatula or spoon shaped.

With its long blooming season and love of damp shade, this is a good perennial herb for the garden. Plant in shade to part shade, with minimum to moderate water or in pots where it can trail over the edge.

Mar–Aug ●
Ma, So, Na, Me
5–60 cm, 2–24 in

Siberian Candyflower

Little Spring Beauty

Claytonia exigua
Purslane Family, *Portulacaceae*

As the name implies this low growing plant is one of the little beauties of spring. Often found growing in dry or sometimes moist soil, in serpentine and chaparral, the contrast between the delicate pink flowers and the fleshy leaves and stems is curious. The flower has five pink petals with tips notched and one opposite pair of dark green lance like leaves fused but partly or fully split on one side. A wildflower that indeed is a beauty to behold.

Apr–Jul ● Ma, So, Na, Me
8–15 cm, 2–6 in

Little Spring Beauty

Miner's Lettuce

Claytonia perfoliata
Purslane Family, *Portulacaceae*

The delicate cluster of tiny flowers above a fleshy, saucer shaped leaf reminds one of a nosegay. This appealing little plant is common to shaded, moist areas and damp trails. Five tiny petals form a cluster of white or pinkish flowers. Leaves initially are paddle shaped but as they grow they completely encircle the stem, becoming umbrella like, with the flower cluster appearing to float above.

This was a favorite food of gold miners since it was a source of vitamin C and prevented scurvy, hence the common name.

This is a good annual herb that reseeds readily and does well in shade to part shade with minimum water. It can spread greatly if given extra water and will develop thick, matted carpets across disturbed areas the first spring. Its shiny black seeds provide food for California quail and other birds.

Feb–May ● Ma, So, Na, Me
10–30 cm, 4–12 in

Miner's Lettuce

Sugarstick
Allotropa virgata
Heath Family, *Ericaceae*

An elusive deep forest dweller, the stalk with its red stripes resembles its common name, Sugarstick. Without chlorophyll to assist in the production of sugars, it extracts sugars and other nutrients from an underground fungus on the roots of nearby trees. The tiny blooms which are tightly attached to the stalk are urn like. On closer look they resemble a bejeweled headdress. Quite an unusual flower.

Jun–Aug ● Ma, So, Na, Me
5–25 cm, 2–10 in

Purple Milkweed

Asclepias cordifolia
Milkweed Family, *Asclepiadaceae*

The reddish purple stem and similarly colored umbel of blooms gives this native milkweed of rocky slopes, chaparral, lava flow and wooded areas its name. Intricate flowers with parts of five and small hoods are typical of *Asclepias*. The leaves clasping the stem are waxy blue. Dried seed pods release tufts of long, silky hairs. Milkweeds have white sap, hence their common name.

A nice herbaceous perennial specimen plant for attracting many insects, including Monarch butterflies. Purple Milkweed needs part to full sun and good drainage to look its best.

May– Jul ● Ma, So, Na, Me
30–90 cm, 1–3 ft

Purple Milkweed

Serpentine Milkweed

Asclepias solanoana
Milkweed Family, *Asclepiadaceae*

The blue green serpentine soils of coastal slopes are the home of this rare species, and hence its name. This ground hugging native milkweed has milky sap and a trailing stem on the ground. The reddish purple, five petal flower balls share the stem with heart shaped opposite pairs of leaves.

Serpentine Milkweed is uncommon in cultivation, and requires excellent drainage in thin soil.

May–Jun ● So, Na, Me
Prostrate

Serpentine Milkweed

Showy Milkweed

Asclepias speciosa
Milkweed Family, *Asclepiadaceae*

This common plant of forests, roadsides, and other varied habitats displays flowers with five rose purple petals and five pinkish, toothlike hoods. The seed pods may be either spiny or smooth and in summer produce seeds with long silky hairs.

The Monarch Butterfly lays its eggs on the underside of this tall plant's oval velvety leaves. The growing larvae then eat the leaves.

Showy Milkweed will form large colonies over time, spreading by underground rhizome, and should be given plenty of room to roam in a large garden setting. A real show stopper when in bloom. Cut back to the ground when it dies back. Prefers full sun and good drainage.

May–Aug ● Ma, So, Na, Me
30–120 cm, 1–4 ft

Beach Sand Verbena
Abronia umbellata
Four O'Clock, *Nyctaginaceae*

A beautiful find in its favored beach habitat, the colorful splash of pink flowers makes a welcome contrast against sandy backgrounds. Sprawling up to 1 m, 3 ft, in length this perennial is generally covered with fine short hairs. The elongated oval leaves are thin but fleshy and attached to the trailing stems. Slender, leafless flower stalks support umbels of 8-20 fragrant rose purple flowers with reddish stems. Individual flowers are trumpet shaped.

Without flowers, this plant may be confused with Yellow Sand Verbena, *A. latifolia*, which has thicker, round to kidney shaped leaves. Upon flowering, there's no chance of confusion.

Most of year ● Ma, So, Me
Stem to 1 m, 3 ft

Beach Sand Verbena

Purple Sanicle
Sanicula bipinnatifida
Carrot Family, *Apiaceae*

Tiny purple or yellow balls of delicate flowers decorate the stalks of this broad leafed Sanicle of open coastal grasslands, woodlands, and chaparral. A leaf with three parts deeply cut and toothed margins. The stem (petiole) between the three parts is broad with a spiny margin.

Purple Sanicle's unusual flower clusters might make it an interesting garden plant in full sun with other low growing plants; it is short lived in cultivation.

Mar–May ● Ma, So, Na, Me
15–60 cm, 6–24 in

Purple Sanicle

Charming Centaury
Centaurium muehlenbergii
Gentian Family, *Gentianaceae*

With "charming" part of this plant's common name, expectations are high that it won't disappoint. This attractive annual, with its branching clusters of distinctive pink to purple flowers and interesting bright green foliage, is definitely appealing. Loose pairs of basal leaves give rise to loosely branching flower stems supporting attractive, star like flowers. Five petals form the white throated flower embracing the stamens with their bright yellow anthers. The entire look is indeed charming.

Charming Centaury is similar to other *Centauriums* and is also known as *Zeltnera muhlenbergii*.

May–Aug ● Ma, So, Na, Me
10–30 cm 4–12 in

Charming Centaury ●

Beach Morning Glory
Calystegia soldanella
Morning-glory Family, *Convolvulaceae*

Beach Morning Glory's large flower petals are five lobed, trumpet shaped in tones of rose purple. The flower stays open most of the day. Leaves are kidney shaped and scattered along the long stem. A common plant to find in sand dunes.

Apr–Aug ● Ma, So, Me
Stem to 50 cm, 20 in

Beach Morning Glory

California Bee Plant

Scrophularia californica
Figwort Family, *Scrophulariaceae*

This long blooming, somewhat tall wildflower can be found flowering from late winter through mid summer in coastal and riparian scrub. Particularly attractive to hummingbirds and bees, the brown to maroon tubular flowers have two projecting upper petals. There are large triangular leaves. In the spring the Bee Plant is especially attractive to deer who will crop off plants to about six inches above the ground.

Medicinally this plant has sedative, astringent, diuretic, and anti fungal properties. It is especially useful as a skin wash.

Feb–Jul ● Ma, So, Na, Me
80–120 cm, 3–4 ft

California Bee-Plant

Snapdragon

Antirrhinum spp.
Figwort Family,
Scrophulariaceae

Opening the "dragon's mouth" of this flower and watching it snap shut has long delighted children of every age. A semi hardy annual, the flowers bloom in shades of white, pink, orange, reds, and yellows, nearly every color except blue. Buds emerge along an erect spike, gradually opening from the bottom to the top. Blossoms are faintly fragrant. Flowers are usually recognizable. There are 4-5 sepals partially united and 4-5 petals united in a two lipped floral tube with 3 lobes down and 2 lobes up. Plants can be dwarf size growing to about 25 cm, 10 in, tall, but more typically are 40–60 cm, 18–24 in tall.

May–Jun ● Ma, So, Na, Me
25–60 cm, 10–24 in

Snapdragon

Chamisso's Hedge Nettle

Hedge Nettle

Hedge Nettle

Stachys ajugoides
Mint Family, *Lamiaceae*

Commonly found in springy ravines and partially shaded canyons, this plant with its exotic looking flowers is a good reason to take up photography. Spiky stems bear opposite pairs of hairy, oblong to egg shaped leaves with scalloped edges. Up to six pink to purple flowers grow in separate whorls along the stem. Petals form two lipped tubular flowers with the lower lip twice as long as the upper and often marked with streaks of a darker color. Even the petals are hairy.

Hedge Nettle will not sting you, but has a pleasant lemon scent if you rub your fingers on the stem.

A generally much taller species, 60-90 cm, 2-3 ft, is Chamisso's Hedge Nettle, *S. chamissonis* (see photo). Found in wet meadows, this plant thrives on moisture in our coastal counties.

May–Sep ● Ma, Me, Na, So
10–100 cm, 2–40 in

Coyote Mint

Monardella villosa ssp. *villosa*
Mint Family, *Lamiaceae*

Common to dry rocky or gravelly areas, you may find this plant covered with butterflies during its summer blooming season. The fragrant, sparsely hairy, gray green leaves and dense clusters of purple to blue purple flowers are certainly attractive. Multiple tiny petals form equally small two lipped floral tubes. From even a short distance the profusion of flowers look colorfully hairy. Leaves are elliptical and fragrantly minty. *Mondardella villosa* is a variable plant with several subspecies.

Spanish settlers used this plant as a cure for sore throats.

A great perennial with very fragrant foliage from summer to fall. Drought tolerant and prefers warm to hot exposure. Needs good drainage or may rot in the winter. Pollinators love it.

Jun–Aug ● Ma, Me, Na, So
to 45 cm, 18 in

Plectritis
Plectritis sp.
Valerian Family, *Valerianaceae*

Cheerful white, pink, to violet flowers standing tall on its erect little stem will be Plectritis, but the species are difficult to identify. Composed of clusters of tiny flowers with five lobed tubular petals atop the stem, the base of each tube is generally spurred or swollen, giving this charming flower a distinct complexity easily enjoyed with a hand lens. Occasionally found on grassy slopes or damp woods.

Apr–Jun ● Ma, So, Na, Me
15–60 cm, 6–24 in

Spanish Lotus
Lotus purshianus
Pea Family, *Fabaceae*

A lovely little native that would be easy to miss with its one pale rose, pea shaped flower. Three compound, lance shaped leaflets are on the long flower stem. A very common plant in disturbed areas.

Apr–Oct ● Ma, So, Na, Me
15–90 cm, 6–36 in

Spanish Lotus

Bicolored Lotus
Lotus formosissimus
Pea Family, *Fabaceae*

The blooms of this native perennial wild pea may be found in moist areas along the coast. Flowers are bicolored, hence the common name, with the banner petal yellow and lower petals pink to purple. The elliptical leaflets are usually five per leaf and seed pods are 3-4 cm, 1-1¹/₂ in, long.

Mar–Jul ● Ma, So, Na, Me
30–60 cm, 1–2 ft

Bicolored Lotus

Tomcat Clover

Trifolium willdenovii
Pea Family, *Fabaceae*

The scientific name *willdenovii* refers to the famous German botanist Carl Ludwig Willdenow (1765-1812). The

common name for this pretty little annual may have been inspired by an imaginative look at the many cat faces in the pinkish and white bloom. This common plant with slender compound leaflets blooms in open grasslands.

Mar–Jun ● Ma, So, Na, Me
15–60 cm, 6–24 in

Tomcat Clover

Cows Clover

Trifolium wormskioldii
Pea Family, *Fabaceae*

This common Pea Family member shows its 3 cm, 1 in, tightly packed whitish and lavender flower head from May through October. Compound leaves are made up of oblong, blunt tipped leaflets. Found in moist places along the coast where one might be likely to find its namesake, cows.

Some sources have this listed as an alien, but our definitive source, Calflora, lists it as a native.

May–Oct ● Ma, So, Na, Me
10–30 cm, 4–12 in

Cows Clover

Milkwort

Polygala californica
Milkwort Family, *Polygalaceae*

This unusual, relatively low growing plant is well worth a close up look. Common to exposed slopes, chaparral and woods, the flowers are quite different. There are three bright to deep pink petals, united at the base, with the lower petal somewhat boat shaped and enclosing the stamens and pistil. There is a resemblance to pea flowers. This slender stemmed perennial is often a bit woody at the base and has elliptical or oblong leaves.

The Latin name means "much milk."

Mar–Jul ● Ma, So, Na, Me
5–35 cm, 2–14 in

Milkwort

Venus Thistle

Cirsium occidentale var. *venustum*
Sunflower Family, *Asteraceae*

The color of the bristly bloom can vary from red to white, pink or purple. This endemic thistle is found on rocky, clayey or sandy soil of grassland and brush. Similar to Cobwebby Thistle, *Cirsium occidentale*, but the head is usually longer than broad, and rarely with the white hairs of Cobbywebby Thistle. Also, generally found further inland.

Apr–Jul ● Ma, So, Na, Me
60–300 cm, 2–10 ft

Venus Thistle

Beach Aster

Lessingia filaginifolia
var. *californica*
Sunflower Family,
Asteraceae

The purplish pink bloom of 30-120 disk flowers of this native perennial can be found on grassy slopes and sand dunes. There are oval shaped, grayish green leaves.

Beach Aster is also known as *Corethrogyne filaginifolia*.

Given moderate summer water and sun, it grows well in gardens. Many butterflies use the nectar.

**Jul–Oct ● Ma, So, Me
to 25 cm, 10 in**

Beach Aster

California Aster

Aster chilensis
Sunflower Family,
Asteraceae

This lovely little flower has a yellow center and white to lavender or pinkish rays. Large lance like leaves are located near the base of the plant with smaller leaves scattered on the stem. You will find this native perennial usually in moist soil.

California Aster out competes other plants, but is good to stabilize or restore disturbed areas and needs only moderate summer water. It is long blooming, a great low grower and pollinator magnet.

**Jun–Aug ● Ma, So, Na, Me
30–122 cm, 1–4 ft**

California Aster

Gilia...
delicate stemmed
fine lobed groves of
suspended pinwheel Goddessettes
flirting

Violet to
Blue

Foothill Penstemon

Penstemon heterophyllus
Figwort Family, *Scrophulariaceae*

This late spring through mid summer wildflower with its deep magenta to vivid blue flower is a beauty to find in our four county region. It favors dry hillsides and rocky cliffs. Five petals united into a two lipped tube form the flower. Stems are smooth and not sticky with linear leaves.

Medicinally the plant has astringent and diuretic properties.

The Foothill Penstemon does well in sunny and dry locations in the garden.

Apr–Jul ● Ma, So, Na, Me
25–150 cm, 10–60 in

Foothill Penstemon

Spinster's Blue Eyed Mary

Collinsia sparsiflora var. *sparsiflora*
Figwort Family, *Scrophulariaceae*

This tiny flower is common to gravelly flats and open grassy places. As the name implies, the blooms are a cluster of tiny blue to lavender and white flowers with the five petals united into a two lipped tube. Similar to other Blue Eyed Marys.

Spinster's Blue Eyed Mary has been used for medicinal purposes.

Favors sunny spots in the garden with good water.

Mar–May ● Ma, So, Na, Me
5–30 cm, 2–12 in

Spinster's Blue Eyed Mary

Round-headed Chinese Houses

Collinsia corymbosa
Figwort Family, *Scrophulariaceae*

A rare endemic to California that grows only on sandy flats or dunes, it is easy to miss this beauty. The purple and white flowers have the five petals united into a two lipped tube of most *Collinsia*, but the flower here is generally more head like than most. The leaf is lance to oval shaped. Growing only on very sandy flats or dunes, it appears in only one coastal area. If you are fortunate to find this rare California wildflower, be sure to take a photo as you may not see it again.

Apr–May ● Me
5–25 cm, 2–10 in

Chinese Houses...
east and west
religion and reason
mysteries meeting in
Buddhist towers
of shady woods

Chinese Houses
Collinsia heterophylla
Figwort Family, *Scrophulariaceae*

This is one of California's most charming wildflowers. Five petals are united into a *Collinsia* style two lipped flower, but here the flowers grow in perfect rings around the stem. They form what look like tiny Chinese pagodas. The lavender, to pale blue to white flowers are nicely complemented by the lance to narrowly triangular foliage. These lovely treasures can be found in shady areas of all four counties.

Chinese Houses favor shade and water in your home garden.

Mar–Jun ● Ma, So, Na, Me
10–50 cm, 4–20 in

California Broomrape

Orobanche californica
Broom-rape Family, *Orobanchaceae*

On dry, rocky soil, near members of the Sunflower Family, look for this very showy purple to white flower. A parasitic perennial that receives its nutrients from various species of the Sunflower Family, this plant has no chlorophyll, and no true leaves. Long petals form floral tubes, 1-5 cm, ¹/₂-2 in, long. The tubes have dark veins, and five long lobes. Many flowers are produced, often in a low level cluster. A real beauty to discover.

May–Aug ● Ma, So, Na, Me
4–35 cm, 1 ¹/₂ –18 in

Clustered Broomrape

Orobanche fasciculata
Broom-rape Family, *Orobanchaceae*

This unusual parasitic perennial completely lacks chlorophyll. It favors dry, generally bare places and is low to the ground. The entire plant, stem, leaves, and flowers, is pale yellow to purple brown in color. The fleshy stem is hairy, wide at the base and narrow toward the tip. There are no true leaves. The petals are long and form tube like flowers in a cluster of stems. The floral tubes have five lobes and bright yellow splotches within the throat.

Apr–Jul ● Ma, So, Na, Me
5–20 cm, 2–8 in

Clustered Broomrape

California Ground Cone

Boschniakia strobilacea
Broom-rape Family, *Orobanchaceae*

What looks like a pine cone in the open woods and chaparral is not related to pines at all. Not often seen by the casual observer, this unusual native plant grows low to the soil. If you see many small reddish brown to dark purplish flowers poking out between the overlapping scales of the flower stalk you've found this parasitic perennial. Favoring Manzanita or Madrone roots, this odd little plant has no leaves nor chlorophyll and must depend on its nearby host. Tiny purple petals form two lipped flowers with five lobes on the plant "cone." You will easily recognize this odd little fellow. The images show a yellow form, which is unusual. A similar plant is Small Ground Cone, *B. hookeri,* typically a smaller plant with a paler color. It is generally found on Salal, *Gaultheria shallon,* in Ma and Me.

May–Jul ● Ma, So, Na, Me
10–30 cm, 4–12 in

California Ground Cone

Hound's Tongue

Cynoglossum grande
Forget-me-not Family,
Boraginaceae

The five petaled, brilliant blue flowers appear atop a 30-90 cm, 1-3 ft, stem on this perennial. A common early blooming spring wildflower of semi shaded places, the wheel like flower has five petals with a hairy leaf that is broadly oval. Hound's Tongue is a lovely plant, getting its name from large broad oval leaves which must have reminded the plant's author of a dog's tongue.

The flower is very similar to other *Cynoglossum, Hackelia,* and the alien *Myosotis sylvatica* or Forget-me-not. The leaves are quite different in all these species.

Hound's Tongue

Mar–Jun ● Ma, So, Na, Me
30–90 cm, 1–3 ft

Swamp Harebell

Campanula californica
Bluebell Family, *Campanulaceae*

The pale blue, five petaled, bell shaped bloom of this miniature plant appears in moist bog like coastal meadows, scrub, and damp forest gaps. The tiny bell points upward. The alternating triangular leaves of this native species are bristling with tiny hairs.

Uncommon in our three coastal counties, Swamp Harebell is listed as rare or endangered by CNPS.

Jun–Sep ● Ma, So, Me
10–30 cm, 4–12 in

Swamp Harebell

Fringed Downingia
Downingia concolor
Bluebell Family, *Campanulaceae*

A soft stem annual that germinates only when inundated with water and temperatures are cool. Downingias are one of an important and unique suite of plant and animal species that have adapted to thrive only within a vernal (seasonally moist then turning completely dry) pool habitat. Lovely little blue or lavender and white bilateral petals with five uneven lobed flowers are a favorite due to their charm. There is a single maroon spot within the large white patch of the lower lip. The linear leaf is tiny.

Two varieties occur within this species: var. *brevior* and var. *concolor*.

Apr–Jul ● So, Na, Me
5–13 cm, 2–5 in

Fringed Downingia

Douglas Iris
Iris douglasiana
Iris Family, *Iridaceae*

This showy perennial is usually found within sight of the ocean on bluffs and grassy hillsides. Stems emerge from clumps of shiny green, blade like leaves with dull green undersides. They are often branched with each branch bearing two or three flowers. Six colorful, elegantly marked petals form a floral tube. Flowers are light blue violet to dark purple but sometimes white and rarely yellow.

Similar to Bowl-tubed Iris, this plant is generally taller with a shorter more open floral tube, and greener leaves.

An excellent perennial for sun to part shade gardens; this plant takes moderate water.

Mar–May ● Ma, So, Na, Me
15–100 cm, 6–36 in

Douglas Iris

Bowl-tubed Iris

Iris macrosiphon
Iris Family, *Iridaceae*

This spring courtier is usually found on open to partly shaded slopes. Plants growing in full sun often have very short stems. Stems emerge individually or from small clumps with blade like leaves. Six elegantly marked petals form a long floral bowl shaped tube. The petals separate near the rim of the floral bowl. Flowers are lavender to deep purple.

I. purdyii x I. macrosiphon

Similar to Douglas Iris, this plant is generally shorter with a much longer bowl like floral tube. Many Iris hybridize and there is an *I. purdyii x I. macrosiphon*.

An excellent perennial for sun to part shade gardens; this plant takes moderate water.

April–Jun ● Ma, So, Na, Me
15–45 cm 6–18 in

Iris purdyii x Iris macrosiphon

Blue-eyed Grass
Sisyrinchium bellum
Iris Family, *Iridaceae*

This delicate grass like perennial with pretty spring flowers favors grassy meadows and hillsides. Six dark veined, blue purple petals form a floral tube that is slightly lighter toward the tip and darker at the center. A bright yellow throat invites curious pollinators. Linear leaves complete this striking low growing jewel. An occasional white form may be seen.

    This is a great small size perennial for borders. It likes sun, and works well in a meadow garden, but do not over water during the summer.

Mar–May ● Ma, So, Na, Me
10–40 cm 4–16 in

Harvest Brodiaea

Brodiaea elegans
Lily Family, *Liliaceae*

Dressed in royal purple petals, this is truly a most elegant, though common, *Brodiaea*. Six shiny deep lavender petals form a funnel shaped flower. Each petal has a prominent mid rib and shades from pale green at the base to white to deep purple at the tip. The flowers are attached to a single, leafless stem in an umbel cluster of up to ten flowers at the top. Found on grassy slopes, hilltops and open woodlands, mounds of grass like basal leaves dry out before the flower appears in late spring.

California Indians baked the bulbs in fire pits and ate them as a vegetable.

Apr–Jul ● Ma, So, Na, Me
20–45 cm, 8–18 in

Harvest Brodiaea

Star Brodiaea

Brodiaea stellaris
Lily Family, *Liliaceae*

The common name of many plants tell a great deal about their dominant features. When viewed from above the striking flower of this perennial does indeed resemble a star. Six blue violet, egg shaped petals form a funnel shaped flower. Three glossy white, forked appendages surround a bundle of deep yellow colored filaments at the center of the flower. Numerous flowers grow in an umbel cluster atop a leafless stem. Leaves are basal and sparse. Look for this attractive endemic plant in serpentine, openings in redwood and mixed evergreen forests. Similar to Harvest Brodiaea, but Star Brodiaea is often smaller.

Apr–Jul ● So, Me
15–25 cm, 6–10 in

Star Brodiaea

Ithuriel's Spear

Triteleia laxa
Lily Family, *Liliaceae*

In mid to late spring as the grasses begin to golden, this bright blue purple flower provides the only contrast color over vast stretches of gold. Spear head like flower buds open to reveal six petals forming each vivid flower. Clusters of flowers sit atop leafless stems. Leaves are basal, linear, and often withered when flowers are present. Common to dry flats, slopes, open woodland, and grassland.

Similar to Harvest Brodiaea, but Ithuriel's Spear has non shiny petals and a longer stem.

Named after the spear of Ithuriel, an angel in Milton's *Paradise Lost*, it is also known as Wally Basket.

Bees and butterflies love this blossom.

Apr–Jun ● Ma, So, Na, Me
30–120 cm, 1–4 ft

Ithuriel's Spear

Ground Brodiaea

Brodiaea terrestris
Lily Family, *Liliaceae*

This perennial grows close to the ground on grasslands near the coast forming small mats. They may be so prevalent it is almost impossible not to step on them. Six shiny, blue violet to pink egg shaped petals with a prominent midrib and tiny spikes at the tip form the typical tube like flower of *Brodiaeas*. Three glossy white, forked appendages surround the center filaments which appear fused together in three segments marked in yellow. The leaves are unremarkable, basal and grass like. The plant is often found among drying grasses.

Apr–Jul ● Ma, So, Na, Me
to 10 cm, 4 in

Ground Brodiaea

Common Camas
Camassia quamash
Lily Family, *Liliaceae*

This useful perennial was well noted in the travel journals of Lewis and Clark. Long vistas of bright blue flowers stretching across wet meadows and the sweet taste of the roasted roots were remarkable to this adventuresome duo. Up close, vivid blue, sometimes white flowers grow in racemes atop thick floral stalks. Each is formed by six petals with one lower petal slightly larger. The leaves are basal and grass like, sometimes 60 cm, 2 ft, in length.

Native Americans called this plant camas or quamash. Roasted bulbs were a delicacy among the Blackfoot, Cree, Nez Pierce and other tribes.

May–Jun ● Ma, So, Na, Me
30–90 cm, 1–3 ft

Common Camas

Blue Dicks
Dichelostemma capitatum
Lily Family, *Liliaceae*

Across meadows and hillsides, in open woodlands, and scrub are dense clusters of blue purple flowers. On their twisted, fleshy, sometimes reddish stems, they wait patiently for flitting pollinators. Six sturdy petals form a bell shaped flower. Leaves are grass like, basal, and unremarkable.

Similar to Ookow, which generally blooms later.

The corms were an important source of starch in the diet of California Indians. Traditional gathering sites were visited annually over long periods of time.

All *Dichelostemmas* are good in containers or meadow gardens. Purchase from a reputable nursery.

Mar–May ● Ma, So, Na, Me
15–46 cm, 6–18 in

Blue Dicks

Ookow

Dichelostemma congestum
Lily Family, *Liliaceae*

In mixed evergreen forest, foothills and open woodlands this blue purple flower can be found blooming in late spring and early summer. Dense clusters of flowers are atop twisted, fleshy stems. Six sturdy petals form a bell shaped flower with petal like stamen appendages. Leaves are grass like, basal, and unremarkable.

Similar to Blue Dicks which generally bloom earlier.

All *Dichelostemmas* are good in containers or meadow gardens. Do not dig in the wild, but purchase from a reputable source.

Apr–Jun ● Ma, Na, So
30–90 cm, 1–3 ft

Ookow

Western Larkspur

Delphinium hesperium
Buttercup Family, *Ranunculaceae*

Even though its blooming season is short, this striking perennial is not easily overlooked. Numerous five petaled white to dark blue purple flowers are on a stalk which can be low to the ground or up to 120 cm, 4 ft, tall. The lobed leaves are maple like and smooth on top but covered with minute hairs underneath.

Scattered throughout California's grassy foothills, this plant favors sunny, dry areas in nature or the western garden.

May–Jun ● Ma, So, Na, Me
15–120 cm, 6–48 in

Western Larkspur

Royal Larkspur

Delphinium variegatum ssp. *variegatum*
Buttercup Family, *Ranunculaceae*

Commonly found on grassy hillsides or open woods, this beautiful Royal Larkspur has very large flowers. The flowers consist of five sepals, the upper one with a prominent spur resembling a dolphin or the spur of a bird; the four petals are inconspicuously placed in the middle. The flower is usually a deep royal purple, but there are rare variations of white or lavender. The leaves are divided into three narrow divisions which fork 3-5 times. This plant blooms early, goes dormant on the hot, dry hillsides of summer, then starts new growth with the cool rains of winter.

Apr–May ● Ma, So, Na, Me
30–60 cm, 1–2 ft

Royal Larkspur

Western Dog Violet

Viola adunca
Viola Family, *Violaceae*

Standing atop an erect stem, this moist meadow perennial has round to heart shaped leaves and dark blue purple flowers. Often found along the banks of streams and creeks or at the dappled edges of sunny meadows.

A useful little plant in your garden, the flowers can be used to make purple dye. Tea made from the dried leaves can be used to treat stomach problems. Nice low growing perennial with fragrant flowers in spring. Likes some sun in winter and at least part shade in summer. Provide moderate water.

Mar–Jul ● Ma, So, Na, Me
5–30 cm, 2–12 in

Western Dog Violet

Bird's-Eye Gilia

Gilia tricolor
Phlox Family, *Polemoniaceae*

One never tires of seeing the beauty of Bird's-Eye Gilia. This fast growing leafy annual blooms heavily in early spring in open grasslands, hills and valleys. The five petals form a small, broad bowl like flower that is lavender and white, with a yellow throat. The pollen is often blue. The leaves are narrow, linear, pinnate.

This is a favorite plant for drying as the shape is interesting and the color will not fade. It should only be taken from gardens and not be picked in the wild.

A great annual for meadow gardens or containers. It prefers full sun and dry conditions. It is easy to grow and can be planted in spring or fall. The fragrant flower attracts hummingbirds and butterflies.

Mar–Apr ● Ma, So, Na, Me
10–40 cm, 4–16 in

Vari-leaf Nemophila

Nemophila heterophylla
Waterleaf Family, *Hydrophyllaceae*

Low mats of tangled green foliage are sometimes easy to take for granted, even when sprinkled with blue or white flowers. But this little charmer is worth a look with a hand lens. The foliage is hairy; from compound leaves, to its stem, the plant is covered with tiny bristly hairs. Against this formidable foliage, five smoothly delicate blue or white petals form broadly bowl shaped flowers. From the throat of the flower five stamens emerge waving little dark anthers inviting pollinators in. You can find this perennial in dappled sunshine and partial shade.

Note that the large foreground leaf is not part of Vari-leaf Nemophila.

Mar–Jul ● Ma, So, Na, Me
10–30 cm 4–12 in

Vari-leaf Nemophila

Baby Blue Eyes

Nemophila menziesii var. *menziesii*
Waterleaf Family, *Hydrophyllaceae*

The bright to pale blue flowers scattered in the spring to summer floral carpets of meadows, grasslands, chaparral, and woodlands are fondly known as Baby Blue Eyes. Low growing and long blooming, these exceptional flowers are enjoyed from afar but appreciated even more so up close. Five petals form a very attractive bowl shaped flower with a white center. The petals are sometimes veined in deeper blue making a lovely contrast with the compound, lobed leaves.

This pretty annual likes part sun to shade and works well in garden containers.

Feb–Jun ● Ma, So, Na, Me
10–30 cm 4–12 in

Baby Blue Eyes

Baby Blue Eyes...
the spring sky
smiling up at itself

Bolander's Phacelia

Phacelia bolanderi
Waterleaf Family, *Hydrophyllaceae*

This low, sprawling, hairy perennial favors disturbed patches within Redwood forests, especially on landslides, around streams, and open coastal slopes. It produces beautiful papery pale blue to lilac flowers. Five petals form a quite showy bell shaped flower that joins with others in loosely coiled cymes. Leaves are large and deeply lobed.

Good spreading perennial ground cover for dry shade, but will take part sun. Nectar is favored by hummingbirds, bees and butterflies; songbirds eat the seeds.

May–July ● Ma, So, Na, Me
30–60 cm 1–2 ft

Bolander's Phacelia

California Phacelia

Phacelia californica
Waterleaf Family, *Hydrophyllaceae*

This sprawling, hairy perennial favors rocky slopes along the California coast. From spring into summer it produces beautiful papery white to blue flowers. Five petals form a quite showy bell shaped flower that joins with others in loosely coiled cymes. Leaves are crinkly, silvery, and compound.

Good spreading perennial ground cover for dry shade but will take part sun. Flowers are blue in late spring. Nectar is favored by hummingbirds, bees and butterflies; songbirds eat the seeds.

Apr–Jul ● Ma, So, Na, Me
30–90 cm 1–3 ft

California Phacelia

Danny's Skullcap

Scutellaria tuberosa
Mint Family, *Lamiaceae*

In shady woods and open brushy areas the fortunate hiker may spot this tiny perennial. Leaves are generally hairy, coarsely toothed, broad ovals. Gently nestled above each of the upper opposite leaves is a violet or blue flower. The petals form a small two lipped tubular flower that up close looks like an old

fashioned Quaker bonnet. Pairs of flowers, which emerge as opposites, will sometimes twist around and appear side by side. This is a plant commonly found after fires.

Mar–Jul ● Ma, Me, Na, So
5–20 cm, 2–8 in

Danny's Skullcap

Chia

Salvia columbariae
Mint Family, *Lamiaceae*

This native annual favors dry, open disturbed sites, chaparral, and coastal scrub. The prominent leaves are compound lobed. Rising from the basal foliage are tall, erect flower stems with head like clusters of spiky bracts holding tiny blue flowers. Bright blue petals form a two lipped floral tube.

The recognized treasure of Chia are the seeds. They were used by Chumash Indians as an energy food for runners carrying messages between villages and as an important food for Native Americans in general. Today, the seeds can be found in many fresh market and health food stores.

Mar–Jun ● Ma, Me, Na, So
10–50 cm, 4–20 in

Chia

Self Heal

Prunella vulgaris
Mint Family, *Lamiaceae*

When you find Self Heal in the moist woods, pastures and roadsides it favors, take a close look at its remarkable flowers. Small purple blue flowers with reddish brown bracts are in an oblong spike. They are formed of two lipped tubes with the upper lip hood like, larger and not lobed; the lower lip is two lobed, often frilly at the tip. Leaves are variable, even on the same plant; elliptical, lance like, rounded or pointed, sometimes with teeth, but almost always hairy.

This perennial is a well known Chinese herb used in Asia and in Western herbal medicine is known for its healing properties.

May–Sep ● Ma, Me, Na, So
10–50 cm, 4–20 in

Vinegar Weed
Trichostema lanceolatum
Mint Family, *Lamiaceae*

Striking blue flowers on short green stems will attract your interest on dry slopes, dry creek beds, and chaparral. But the oil rich foliage of this vinegar scented annual can assail your senses when the weather heats up. The numerous leaves are green and hairy, and the toxic properties of the oil they contain keep other plant species from competing for its space. Five bright blue petals form a two lipped tubular flower on a square stem. The flower tube is curved abruptly upward near the throat.

Similar to Turpentine Weed, *T. laxum*, but the lower stalks of its leaves are longer, greater than 5 mm, 1/8 in.

Native Americans used this plant as a cold and fever remedy, and as a flea repellent in bed rolls, as did cowboys.

A good companion to other sun loving, drought resistant natives.

Two forms of Vinegar Weed are shown here.

Apr–Aug ● Ma, So, Na, Me
10–60 cm 4–24 in

Many-colored Lupine

Lupinus varicolor
Pea Family, *Fabaceae*

This common Lupine of many coastal habitats also blooms in many different colors, hence the name *varicolor*. White, yellow, rose or purple flowers may be seen on this shrubby perennial with palmately compound leaves. You may find this in grassy fields and dunes. Similar to other Lupines.

Apr–Jul ● Ma, So, Me

20–50 cm, 8–20 in

Many-colored Lupine

Sky Lupine

Lupinus nanus
Pea, *Fabaceae*

This common annual Lupine may be found in fields and grassy areas of the North Coast Ranges. The petals are typically a beautiful blue, rarely light blue, lavender, pink, or white, and are set off with a white spot on the banner. Flowers are usually whorled. The plant is generally hairy, with palm like compound leaves. Similar to other Lupines, especially *L. affinis* which is nearly identical.

Apr–May ● Ma, So, Na, Me
10–60 cm, 4–24 in

Sky Lupine

Bicolored Lupine

Lupinus bicolor
Pea Family, *Fabaceae*

Grassy slopes are home to this lupine with tiny
.5 mm, ¹/₄ in, deep blue flowers. The banner petal
is oblong with a squared top and a white spot.
The palmate leaves are hairy above and similar to
other Lupines.

Mar–Jun ● Ma, So, Na, Me
15–40 cm, 6–16 in

Bicolored Lupine

Lupine

Lupinus spp.
Pea Family, *Fabaceae*

The genus name *Lupinus* is from the Latin *lupus*, wolf, because this plant,
which often grows in poor soils, was thought to steal vitality from the ground.
All are members of the Pea Family and are actually "nitrogen fixers" which
transform nitrogen from the atmosphere into ammonia, a type of fertilizer.
The palm like, finely haired leaves and pea shaped flowers are characteristic of
this genus. The flowers produce a hairy pod in late summer. Colorful blooms
range from white, yellow, blue to purple. Common in many of our habitats,
Lupine may be an annual, perennial, or shrub. As the breeze blows on hot
summer days the rattling of seeds in their pods may be heard.

Mar–Aug ● Ma, So, Na, Me
Varies

Silver Bush Lupine

Lupine in bud

Periwinkle

Vinca major
Dogbane Family, *Apocynaceae*

The pinwheel like purple blooms of this invasive, non native, weed are seemingly ubiquitous. A folk tale tells of this vine like annual's seeds being spread by the wagon wheels of the Padres in Mission California in the 1700's. However, in California Periwinkle does not reproduce by seed in the wild. It spreads quickly by means of its prostrate stems which root at the tips. Most often it

is found in areas of old homesites, often growing in patches around the bases of trees. It spreads up and down drainages where the cover may be dense. It causes displacement of native species, erosion and bank destabilization, and is a host for the insect pests Sharpshooters which carry a pathogen of vineyards and orchards. Cal-IPC rates this plant as B in impact, distribution, and invasiveness. This is **not** a plant for the garden.

Periwinkle ●

Mar– Jul ● Ma, So, Na, Me
30–60 cm, 1–2 ft

Purple Nightshade

Solanum xanti
Night Shade Family, *Solanaceae*

This medium to tall perennial has 3 cm, 1 in, wide violet to purple flowers and dark green foliage. Its five lobed cup like flower of fused petals, attracts hummingbirds, bees, and butterflies to gather the nectar. Preferring woodlands, Purple Nightshade can often be found under oak trees or in shrub lands.

The long blooming season makes this flower somewhat common to the casual hiker. But be careful, many plants in this family are toxic. The Purple Nightshade is **poisonous** and should not be consumed in any form, including the small green berries. For this reason, the plant is not invited into the garden.

Feb–Jul ● Ma, So, Na, Me
40–90 cm, 15–36 in

Purple Nightshade

Seaside Daisy

Erigeron glaucus
Sunflower Family,
Asteraceae

The native Seaside Daisy decorates the bluffs and dunes of the coastal strand with patches of purple. This perennial herb has flower heads of about 100 lavender ray flowers and yellow disk flowers. Its leaves are widely egg shaped to spoon shaped. Seaside Daisy seeks out sunny spaces and brightens them even more.

Apr–Aug ● Ma, Me, Na, So
10–40 cm, 4–16 in

Brown to Green

Fragrant Fritillary

Fritillaria liliacea
Lily Family, *Liliaceae*

This early blooming harbinger of spring is rare with a limited distribution. It shares the late winter floral spotlight with Mission Bells, but the two grow in very different habitats. This plant, when found, is in an open grassland habitat, and grows in heavy clay soils. Six petals form the green striped white flowers which usually grow in loose racemes of two or a few flowers. The flowers often face outward or nod downward. Leaves are alternate along the lower stem, linear or egg shaped.

Fresh cooked roots were eaten by Native Americans or dried for later use.

All *Fritillarias* are good bulbs for the garden or in containers. Plants should be grown from seed or purchased from reputable bulb growers.

Feb–Apr ● Ma, So
4–14 cm, 3–6 in

Fragrant Fritillary

Mission Bells

Fritillaria affinis
Lily Family, *Liliaceae*

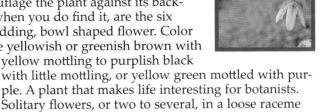

This perennial is common among oaks and brush, but you must look carefully to find it. The brownish color of its blossoms tends to camouflage the plant against its background. Most striking, when you do find it, are the six pointed petals of this nodding, bowl shaped flower. Color varies greatly and can be yellowish or greenish brown with yellow mottling to purplish black with little mottling, or yellow green mottled with purple. A plant that makes life interesting for botanists. Solitary flowers, or two to several, in a loose raceme are borne by sturdy stems with leaves in whorls. Another common name is Checker Lily.

Native Americans cooked and ate the roots.

All *Fritillarias* are good bulbs for the garden or in containers, but should never be dug from the wild. See Resources for purchasing.

Feb–May ● Ma, So, Na, Me
10 cm–1 1/5 m, 1–3 3/4 ft

Mission Bells

Mission Bells
the sound in the forest
no one's around to hear

Chocolate Lily

Fritillaria biflora var. *biflora*
Lily Family, *Liliaceae*

A yummy sounding perennial bulb that is a California endemic. It is also known as Roderick's Fritillary, *F. roderickii,* and with that name is listed by CNPS as an endangered species. An uncommon spring blooming plant, it has six thick, chocolate colored petals forming nodding, bell shaped flowers. The inside is lined with green and purple. But as with Mission Bells, *F. biflora,* they tend to vary in color. Alternate leaves are linear to narrow and oval. Preferring heavy clay soils on open grassy slopes and coastal flats, this long blooming plant is also called Mission Bells.

Feb–Jun ● So, Na, Me
15– 45 cm, 6–18 in

Purdy's Fritillary

Fritillaria purdyi
Lily Family, *Liliaceae*

This rare, striking beauty has limited distribution and is endemic to California. When found, it is growing on serpentine, dry ridges, and chaparral where it has little competition. Like many other *Fritillarias*, the flowers are striking with their highly mottled coloration and grow in loose racemes of one to several on a single stem. The six petals forming the bowl shaped flower are white and generously freckled with brown to purple markings. The base of the petals are lightly dusted with pink and complemented by deep pink on the stamens. Somewhat thick, broad leaves are linear to oval, generally basal and tend to fold gently inward on this short, squat perennial.

Mar–Jun ● Na, Me
10–38 cm, 4–15 in

Purdy's Fritillary

Slink Pod

Scoliopus bigelovii
Lily Family, *Liliaceae*

This unusual Lily, common to moist, shady banks and Redwood forests, could easily be missed if not for its large basal purple mottled leaves. From the center of the leaves 2-12 eye

catching flowers emerge on thin brown stalks. Flowers of pale green have vivid deep maroon lines. After pollination, the weight of the swelling seed pod bends the stalk onto the ground, hence its Slink Pod name. Blossoms are ill scented when fresh, for another common name of Fetid Adder's Tongue. This plant may be the first bloomer of the year.

Feb–Mar ● Ma, So, Na, Me
8–20 cm, 3–8 in

Slink Pod

California Lady's Slipper

Cypripedium californicum
Orchid Family, *Orchidaceae*

This rare plant has a very unusual flower. Favoring wet hillsides and rocky ledges, you may find it growing in a tall clump. Leaves are oval, alternate, 5-15 cm, 2-6 in long. The floral stem may hold up to twelve small flowers. Each flower has yellow green sepals and mostly white petals. But the lower petal, the lip, gives this plant its name. It is significantly larger than the other flower parts and looks like a pillow, balloon, or slipper.

May–Jun ● Ma, So, Me
30–120 cm, 1–4 ft

California Lady's Slipper

Coastal Piperia

Piperia elegans
Orchid Family,
Orchidaceae

This Orchid has white greenish flower parts and a long flower spike that takes up at least half the height of the plant. The flowers have two petals, and three petal like sepals with dark green veins and a long spur pointed down. Numerous flowers grow in a spike. The plant has 2-5 linear, basal leaves which are often already dried up at flowering. You may find Coastal Piperia in dry open sites. Also known as *Habenaria elegans*.

All Orchids have a symbiotic relationship with fungi that make it difficult to use in native gardens. Never dig plants from the wild.

May–Sep ● Ma, So, Na, Me
to 30 cm, 1 ft

Coastal Piperia

Royal Rein Orchid

Piperia transversa
Orchid Family, *Orchidaceae*

Royal Rein Orchid

Found in partial shade to full sun, in dry oak or mixed conifer woods and coastal forests, this prolific bloomer can have a hundred white to greenish flowers along its flower spike. Rising from a pair of basal leaves which wither at bloom time, the spike gingerly holds its flowers in a show of floral confidence. Each flower has the two petals and three petal like sepals, typical of the Orchid Family, with an atypical long flattened spur. Both sepals and petals have a green mid vein. At night, its sweet floral fragrance perfumes the air.

Similar to Coastal Piperia, the flower spur differentiates this plant.

Jun–Aug ● Ma, So, Na, Me
15–50 cm, 6–20 in

Gnome Plant

Hemitomes congestum
Heath Family,
Ericaceae

Gnome Plant

The Gnome Plant is so secretive and illusive one is as likely to encounter a forest gnome as see one of these deep forest dwellers. They are almost hidden in the humus of the coniferous forest floor. The tan cream colored, cylindrical flowered clumps produce no chlorophyll but rather extract nutrients from decaying matter. The short lived blooms appear in May and June and soon decompose into black gooey masses.

May–Jun ● Ma, So, Me
3–10 cm, 1–4 in

Pickleweed

Salicornia virginica
Goosefoot Family,
Chenopodiaceae

Call it what you will, Pickleweed, Glasswort, Swampfire or Salt Horn (*Salicornia*). This native plant of salty coastal flats is an overlooked member of the coastal plant community. The long, creeping, green, water filled, succulent stems of this annual turn a rusty red in the autumn months. The salt filled ends die and fall off. Tiny spike petalled flowers and scale like leaves are found in the stem segment joints.

Also known as *Sarcocornia pacifica*.

Aug–Nov ● Ma, So, Na, Me
to 120 cm, 4 ft

Pickleweed

Dwarf Plantain

Plantago erecta
Plantain Family,
Plantaginaceae

This low growing annual is commonly found on loose sandy or gravelly soil of coastal bluffs to grassy hills and wooded canyons. Although the petals are colorless, they are quite attractive in their translucent beauty. Four minute petals compose the flower; they are concave, pointed at the tip and bend downward from the flower center. Flowers grow in spikes with the leaves linear, covered with long, soft hairs growing in a cluster at the base of the plant.

This plant is a nice addition to the native garden, does not require water in summer, and can be used to restore degraded areas.

Mar–May ● Ma, So, Na, Me
5–15 cm, 2–6 in

Dwarf Plantain

Pacific Seaside Plantain

Plantago maritima
Plantain Family,
Plantaginaceae

Occasionally found on coastal bluffs and saline habitats, this slender spiky perennial is interesting. The colorless flowers have four minute petals. They are wind pollinated and grow in tight spikes on the ends of long leafless flower stalks. When the yellow anthers hang out from the flowers on the ends of their long filaments to produce pollen, they look like tiny satellites. Leaves are linear, fleshy and channeled with veins. This is probably why it is also called Goose Tongue, if you've chanced to see one.

The seeds are very small but were ground into powder and used as a flour extender by California Indians.

June–Aug ● Ma, So, Na, Me
5–23 cm, 2–9 in

Pacific Seaside Plantain

Turkey Mullein

Eremocarpus setigerus
Spurge Family, *Euphorbiaceae*

Tiny white petal rosettes adorn this low growing annual of dry open spaces. More striking than the blooms are the heavily scented, gray green leaves in a rosette. The fluffy delicate feel of the leaves may give this plant one of its common names, Dove Weed.

The Spurge Family has some interesting members, including Poinsettias and Castor-bean, whose seeds yield castor oil.

May–Oct ● Ma, So, Na, Me
3–20 cm, 1–8 in

Turkey Mullein

Stinging Nettle

Urtica dioica ssp. *holosericea*
Nettle Family, *Urticaceae*

This mid to late summer blooming perennial will be easily identified after the first encounter. But it is not the flowers that will grab your attention. They are tiny and mostly indistinguishable clusters growing above the lance shaped leaves. It is the stinging hairs on the toothed leaves and stems that will remind you to give this common, damp area plant a bit of respectful distance. The hairs contain a skin reactive poison that can cause severe stinging which may last for hours.

Red Admiral and West Coast Lady butterflies use species of *Urtica* as a larval food plant. In a habitat garden this may be a plant to consider.

Jun–Sep ● Ma, So, Na, Me
1–2 m, 3–7 ft

Stinging Nettle

Wild Ginger

Asarum caudatum
Pipevine Family, *Aristolochiaceae*

The flower of this low growing native smells gingery and is found in deep wood habitats. Wild Ginger has no true petals, but three beautiful deep maroon sepals that are hidden under heart shaped leaves with pointed ends.

Wild Ginger is a slow growing ground cover for use in deep shade to part sun, with some supplemental summer water required. The exotic flowers are pollinated by slugs and ants serving as assistants in the dispersal of this plant's seeds.

May–Jul ● Ma, So, Na, Me
3–15 cm, 1–6 in

Wild Ginger

Fringe Cups

Tellima grandiflora
Saxifrage Family, *Saxifragaceae*

This beautiful plant is a delight to find in shaded woods. Slender wands of cuplike flowers with short green to rose petals that are fringed on the tips, attract your attention above the rich green, maple like foliage. The unusual petals change from green to cream, to deep pink or brown red as they age.

In the garden, Fringe Cups favor shade and water.

Apr–Jun ● Ma, So, Na, Me
30–90 cm, 1–3 ft

Fringe Cups

Woolly Marbles

Psilocarphus tenellus var. *tenellus*
Sunflower Family, *Asteraceae*

The greenish gray blooms of this low growing, prostrate annual appear in April. The native Woolly Marbles is very common on dry slopes with generally disturbed soil, rarely vernal pools. It grows in low clumps with its tiny, cobwebby, woolly balls. The leaves are small, linear. A tiny plant that is worth a closer look.

Apr–June ● Ma, So, Na, Me
3–10 cm, 1–4 in

Woolly Marbles

Calypso Orchid...
out of the limelight
delicate dancer on
soft, damp soil

Ferns & Grasses

Giant Chain Fern
Woodwardia fimbriata
Deer Fern Family,
Blechnaceae

From their primordial beginnings these dwellers of forest stream banks have decorated the coastal forests for millennia. One might imagine a dinosaur cruising amidst large patches of this largest of North American ferns. Little raised bumps or bundles, called sori, form patterns on the underside of the fronds resembling the links of a chain, hence the common name Chain Fern.

The stalks were used by Native Americans to make baskets.

This fern is lovely in woodland setting with its large, beautiful fronds. Happiest near water.

● Ma, So, Na, Me
1–3 m, 3–10 ft

Giant Chain Fern

Western Bracken Fern
Pteridium aquilinum var. *pubescens*
Bracken Family, *Dennstaedtiaceae*

A very common fern of many habitats, but particularly moist areas in open meadows. Sometimes an indicator species for archaeologists as the Western Bracken Fern grows in disturbed areas and old building sites are outlined by these ferns. Linear oblong leaf segments are part of a frond. This fern is deciduous, dying back in late summer.

The core of the long creeping underground black rhizomes were used by California Indians in basket design. The juice extracted from young fronds was used as a body deodorant.

● Ma, So, Na, Me
15–150 cm, ½–5 ft

Western Bracken Fern

California Wood Fern

Dryopteris arguta
Wood Fern Family, *Dryopteridaceae*

Fittingly, the name of this coastal plant is derived from the Greek *dryo* oak, *pteris* fern and *arguta* meaning sharp toothed. This lacy fern can be seen growing under oaks and bays in shady coastal canyons, particularly among sandstone boulders. Occasionally the leaf may be up to 105 cm, 3¹/₂ ft, long.

Beautiful evergreen fern in the garden with shade to part shade and low to medium water.

California Wood Fern

● Ma, So, Na, Me
30–60 cm, 1–2 ft

Western Sword Fern

Polystichum munitum
Wood Fern Family, *Dryopteridaceae*

Western Sword Fern is named for the tiny hilt on the under side of the shiny green leaf blade. This fern grows in sometimes massive clumps in Redwood and mixed Douglas-fir forests. Round spore cases are arranged in rows on the underside.

The fronds were used by California Indians to line the leaching pits for acorn preparation along river banks.

Excellent evergreen fern that likes shade to part shade and medium to regular water. Provides good visual structure.

● Ma, So, Na, Me
45–105 cm, 18–42 in

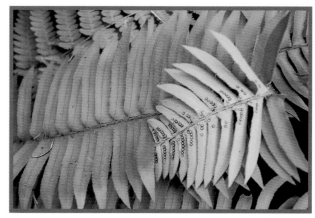

Western Sword Fern

Lady Fern

Athyrium filix-femina
Wood Fern Family, *Dryopteridaceae*

Lady Fern

The delicate lacy cut leaflets of this common fern of meadows, fields, woods and ravines evokes the gentle ethereal feel of a true fern. A delight to behold in any habitat. The underside spore cases are pale and j shaped. The lacy, twice cut fronds are a distinguishing feature.

Not surprisingly this was a favorite fern of Victorian ladies, and the name comes from the Latin *filix-femina* for fern-feminine.

Pretty deciduous fern for the garden. Likes shade to part shade and medium to regular water.

● Ma, So, Na, Me
61–90 cm, 24–36 in

California Polypody

Polypodium californicum
Brake Family, *Pteridaceae*

This creeping perennial fern is commonly found in rock crevices, shaded canyons, and seeps in coastal areas. It is sometimes epiphytic, deriving its nutrients from rain, air, dust, etc. It particularly favors the shade of Live Oaks. A deciduous native, the leaves emerge in late fall with the first rains. As the ground dries out in summer, the plant goes dormant until the rains return. The underside of each frond is lined with distinct rows of round spore cases.

Native Americans used this plant to treat wounds and rheumatism.

Lovely deciduous fern that likes shade to part shade and minimum to occasional water. Browsed by wildlife.

● Ma, So, Na, Me
10–25 cm, 4–10 in

California Polypody

Coffee Fern

Pellaea andromedifolia
Brake Family, *Pteridaceae*

Generally found on dry, rocky slopes in woods, this interesting plant has the typical shape of a fern frond. But the shape of the leaves are rounded like a coffee bean. Turn the leaf over to see the spore case and find it outlining the edge of each leaf. The bean like leaves are attached to loosely branched reddish stems. Together they make up a frond. A long creeping rhizome with small tan to orange brown scales with a darker mid stripe that enhances the coffee bean image.

- Ma, So, Na, Me
  to 20 cm, 8 in

Coffee Fern

Indian's Dream

Aspidotis densa
Brake Family, *Pteridaceae*

Appearing like star bursts of bright green against a rocky background, this low growing fern is commonly found in rock crevices, on outcrops, often on serpentine, sometimes in chaparral. It brightens the landscape with leaf blades that are bright green, compound, and somewhat leathery. Fertile leaves stand more erect than sterile leaves and their blades are narrower.

- Ma, So, Na, Me
  15–20 cm, 6–8 in

Indian's Dream

Common Grapefern

Botrychium multifidum
Adder's-tongue Family, *Ophioglossaceae*

This low growing fern is found in sunny meadows, forest clearings and at the edges of marshes. The leaf blades are a little larger than others in the genus, and rather fleshy and leathery. New fronds appear in July through August among the yellowed remains of the previous year's fronds. The sterile frond is a single bright green broadly triangular leaf with a long stem holding densely clustered and overlapping leaflets. The fertile frond is widely branched; often erect and almost stalk like. Its spore cases resemble grapes clustered along the stem.

- Ma, So, Me
  to 20 cm, 8 in

Common Grapefern

Giant Horsetail

Equisetum telmateia ssp. *braunii*
Horsetail Family, *Equisetaceae*

When dinosaurs roamed parts of western North America they strolled among, and many maybe munched upon, forebears of this ancient species. *Equisetum* is considered the oldest vascular plant genus. Erect stems of two different sorts, one sterile and resembling an erect horse's tail, or asparagus shoots, with tiny tube like fronds sticking out from a central shoot. The other stem is fertile, pale, and unbranched. These prehistoric plants are frequently found in moist soil, woods, and thickets. Other *Equisetum* species are similar with Common Horsetail, *E. arvense* being smaller, more delicate and flexible.

May be toxic to young horses and sheep.

Mar–May ● Ma, So, Na, Me
fertile 15–46 cm, 6–18 in
sterile 30–100 cm, 12–40 in

Giant Horsetail

Salt Rush
Juncus lesueurii
Rush Family, *Juncaceae*

This grass like perennial is generally found along the borders of salt or fresh-water marshes, usually near dunes along the coast. Leaves are basal with narrow blades and light brown sheaths. Prominent spiky bracts enfold the less prominent flower. The two lowest bracts resemble the stem. Flowers are somewhat indistinguishable from the foliage in their brown, green coloration and dark margins. A very unusual flower that may entice you to visit the marshes.

May–Aug ● Ma, So, Na, Me
30–140 cm, 1–4 ¹/₂ ft

Salt Rush ●

Naked Sedge
Carex nudata
Sedge Family, *Cyperaceae*

Clumps of this perennial flowering sedge appear in the rocky soils of stream banks. The showy black flower spikes appear in winter/early spring. The female flower is surrounded by an urn shaped bract that persists into the winter, turning orangish during the fall and dark brown in winter.

Can be grown in pots or in shallow water.

Mar–Apr ● Ma, So, Na, Me
to 76 cm, 30 in

Naked Sedge

Salt Grass

Salt Grass

Distichlis spicata
Grass Family, *Poaceae*

This native perennial grass is common in salt marshes, brackish coastal marshes, and saline flats. It grows to 50 cm, 20 in, tall as straw colored erect stems with purplish leaf blades all along the stem.

An important food source for geese and other migrating birds, several species of butterflies depend on this plant for larval food.

Because this plant secretes microscopic salt crystals on its leaf blades and stems, it is currently being tested for its potential to reclaim salinated soils for agricultural use.

Apr–Jul ● Ma, So, Na, Me
10–50 cm, 4–20 in

California Fescue

Festuca californica
Grass Family, *Poaceae*

This beautifully proportioned bunch grass is distributed from wet coastal areas to wooded slopes and chaparral, and often seen under oaks. The blue green foliage is graceful and fountain like and stays green all year along the coast. Airy, feather like flowers unfurl on stems that rise as much as an additional 61 cm, 2 ft, above the dense basal foliage.

This is an excellent ground cover for slopes and grows well in sun and partial shade. It is drought tolerant, but with minimal to medium water in summer will stay green throughout the year. An excellent medium tall clumping grass.

Apr–Jul ● Ma, So, Na, Me
46–122 cm, 18–48 in

California Fescue

Pampas Grass

Cortaderia jubata
Grass Family, *Poaceae*

This perennial grass is a problematic, non native, invasive weed! Its huge nodding pinkish to deep violet flower plumes turn creamy white when mature and rise up to three times higher than the foliage clump. The bright to deep green leaf has razor like margins. This plant is found only in coastal areas, along Highway 1 in roadside cuts, forest clear cuts, mud slides, or burned areas.

C. jubata produces abundant seeds annually and establishes quickly on bare soil. Spread occurs by wind blown seed or by humans using mature plumes in decorative arrangements or using plants in landscaping. Seeds have been reported to disperse over twenty miles under windy conditions. Native coastal ecosystems are crowded out and native plant diversity is affected. All seed production occurs without pollen transfer with little genetic diversity existing within plants, which may explain its limited range in California.

Because of its highly invasive and competitive characteristics, it is rated A in impact, distribution, and invasiveness by Cal-IPC. Don't even think about putting this in your garden or picking the plumes!

Jul–Sep ● Ma, So, Me
1.8–7 m, 6–23 ft

Vines, Shrubs & Trees

Poison Oak

Toxicodendron diversilobum
Sumac Family, *Anacardiaceae*

This much maligned native vine or shrub displays beautiful red foliage in late summer to fall. Flowers are greenish white to cream with five loosely clustered petals. With three leaflets and an upper surface that is shiny, this is one plant that everyone should learn to identify. Many people develop dermatitis from Poison Oak as even brushing against the leaves or leafless stem can cause a rash. Do not burn the plant, as the poison can be inhaled. Growing in many habitats, the leaves are similar to young oak trees, hence, the common name. Whitish berries are a help, when in fruit, for further distinction between oak and Poison Oak.

California Indians used the sap as a dye for basketry and in tattooing. It was also used as a wart cure.

Not commonly planted, this plant does provide valuable shelter and food for many wildlife species. Birds enjoy the berries.

Poison Oak

Apr–May ● Ma, So, Na, Me
Vine to 25 m, 85 ft; Shrub .6–4 m, 2–14 ft

Dutchman's Pipe

Aristolochia californica
Pipevine Family, *Aristolochiaceae*

The musty fragrance of fungus given off by the veined, brown green, pipe shaped flowers attracts insects which fertilize these enchanting woody vines. The flower is unmistakable in bloom with the petals and sepals fused into a sack with a lid. Heart to arrow shaped leaves are on the variable crawling or climbing vine found along stream sides, in forests or chaparral.

In the garden, Dutchman's Pipe can be slow growing at first, but will grow quickly once established. One of a few plants in which the flower starts out in miniature and then grows to its final size during the bloom period. These plants will often become deciduous in summer if not watered, awakening with the first rains. Tolerates full sun in cooler areas, but needs shade in heat. The beautiful Pipevine Swallowtail butterfly lays its eggs exclusively on *Aristolochia*. The larval stage of the beautiful butterfly uses the plant for food.

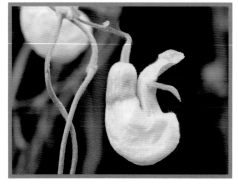

Dutchman's Pipe

Jan–Apr ● Ma, So, Na, Me
30–90 cm, 1–3 ft

Pink Honeysuckle

Lonicera hispidula var. *vacillans*
Honeysuckle Family, *Caprifoliaceae*

This lovely common vine of stream courses and wooded hillsides shows pink tubelike flowers with five unequal lobes. The leaf is oblong to ovate. The climbing variety can be seen rambling through Coyote Brush and other local shrubs and frequently attracts hummingbirds. The red berries of this native shrub are consumed by many passing birds.

The hollow stems were used by California Indians as pipe stems and ashes of the burned woody stem were crushed into a paste for tattooing.

Pink Honeysuckle will grow in sun and shade, without much water, but requires support.

Apr–Jul ● Ma, So, Na, Me
1.5–6 m, 5–20 ft

Pink Honeysuckle

Twinberry

Lonicera involucrata
Honeysuckle Family,
Caprifoliaceae

A treat to behold in many moist coastal habitats, this shrub with elliptical leaves produces twin yellow tubular flowers cupped in green bracts. The glossy deep purple double berries ripen near summer's end and are presented in a cup of now bright maroon bracts appearing as a reddish ruff of Tudor women's dress. A delight to the eye but brutally bitter to the taste.

Mar–Jun ● Ma, So, Na, Me
.9–1.8 m, 3–6 ft

Twinberry

Yerba Santa

Eriodictyon californicum
Waterleaf Family, *Hydrophyllaceae*

This very drought tolerant evergreen shrub can be found in the drier areas of fields and woodlands. Sometimes quite tall with a branched woody stem, it is a treat to encounter during its blooming season. The funnel shaped, white to lavender flowers have four petals and a very lovely scent. Leaves are simple, lance shaped, and alternate. They are leathery with a sticky or hairy upper surface and a lower surface that is densely covered with short matted woolly hairs.

Native Americans used this plant as a cure all. Many cough medicines today count it as an ingredient.

In the landscape it is often used to stabilize soil along loose banks to prevent erosion.

May–Jul ● Ma, So, Na, Me
1–3 m, 3–9 ft

Yerba Santa

Pipestems

Clematis lasiantha
Buttercup Family, *Ranunculaceae*

This woody deciduous vine with its charming flowers of four pointed stars climbs shrubs and trees along hillsides, chaparral, and open woodlands. The creamy flowers grow in clusters of 1-3 from the green foliage of compound leaves are attractive. But the masses of seed carrying plumes which emerge as the flowers mature really catch the eye. A similar plant, Virgin's Bower, *C. ligusticifolia*, grows with larger flower clusters and blooms Jun-Sep.

Native Americans mashed the leaves and bark to make medicinal soap and shampoo, and boiled the leaves to apply to sores and rashes. Tea was made from its leaves or bark for headaches, sore throats and fevers. Dried seed floss is an excellent tinder and the stems have been used to make string.

Very easy in the garden in a moist spot with part to full sun.

Jan–Jun ● Ma, So, Na, Me
1–10 m, 3–35 ft

Pipestems

Western Thimbleberry
Rubus parviflorus
Rose Family, *Rosaceae*

This member of the Rose Family is commonly found growing on moist slopes and stream banks as a vine or shrub. The five petaled flowers with many stamens, typical of the roses, grow in clusters of 4-7 white to pink flowers among

large, lightly prickly, maple like deciduous leaves. As their name implies, the salmon colored fruits are thimble like, looking much like raspberries.

In the garden, Western Thimbleberry likes shade and a little water.

Mar–Aug ● Ma, So, Na, Me
to 2 m, 6 ft

California Wild Grape
Vitis californica
Grape Family, *Vitaceae*

A somewhat aggressive spreading vine that favors stream sides, springs, and canyons. Yellow flowers with five petals grow in clusters and attract butterflies, birds and particularly bees. The lance shaped leaves may have up to three indented margins. They are green on top, gray green underneath, and fuzzy. In late summer the fruit ripens. The small grapes provide late fall and winter food for wildlife.

The vine is grown as an ornamental, often for its large brilliant colored leaves in fall. A vigorous growth habit and it is gorgeous on a trellis or arbor. Prune annually to control. Loved by wildlife.

**May–Jun ● Ma, So, Na, Me
to 9 m, 30 ft**

California Wild Grape

Apocynum sp.

Indianhemp Dogbane
Apocynum cannabinum
Dogbane Family,
Apocynaceae

The small, whitish pink, bell shaped flowers are scattered in clusters among erect pairs of lance shaped leaves. Moist, well drained meadows and stream banks provide fine locations for this shrub.

Other members of the Dogbane Family are very similar and hybridize, specifically with Spreading Dogbane, *A. androsaemifolium*, in our area.

A source of fiber for Native Americans.

Indianhemp Dogbane requires a constant supply of moisture throughout the year, and can become invasive wherever enough water exists.

**Jun–Sep ● Ma, So, Na, Me
30–120 cm, 1–4 ft**

Indianhemp Dogbane

Coyote Brush, male flowers ●

Coyote Brush, female flowers

Coyote Brush

Baccharis pilularis
Sunflower Family, *Asteraceae*

The native Coyote Brush lives up to its name for its variable range and variable appearances from prostrate to erect. Plants are "leggy" and the leaves are clustered at the ends of long stems. Flower heads are white or yellow in tight clusters. Evergreen leaves are three veined, simple to toothed. Shrubs are either male or female and are found from the seashore through the coastal hills to the grasslands and chaparral. The fluffy tailed seeds are spread by wind dispersion.

It is used in restoration and as a ground cover. Coyote Brush needs excellent drainage with minimum to moderate summer water.

Aug–Dec ● Ma, So, Na, Me
to 3 m, 10 ft

Mule Fat

Baccharis salicifolia
Sunflower Family,
Asteraceae

The native shrub, Mule Fat, likes canyon bottoms, stream sides and wetlands. This willow like member of the Sunflower Family has yellow male and white female blooms on separate bushes. There are also two seasonal forms. Summer forms have terminal flower clusters and toothed leaves. Winter forms have lateral flower clusters and toothless leaves. Its leaves are willow like.

**Apr–Oct ● Ma, So, Na, Me
to 30 cm, 12 ft**

Mule Fat, male flowers

Spicebush

Calycanthus occidentalis
Spicebush Family, *Calycanthaceae*

This bushy shrub is found along creeks and coastal canyons. Opposing elliptic or oblong fragrant leaves appear from the brown bark on erect branches. Individual reddish brown colored flowers appear at the end of the branches and are in bloom through the summer months.

California Indians used the bark for brewing a tea to cure chest colds and sore throats.

The native Spicebush grows in sun or part shade, likes water, and the shrub can be pruned into a small tree.

**Apr–Aug ● So, Na, Me
1–3 m, 3–10 ft**

Spicebush

Blue Elderberry
Sambucus mexicana
Honeysuckle Family, *Caprifoliaceae*

Blue Elderberry is a common native shrub which grows in forest clearings and stream banks. Small white to yellowish, five lobed flowers in large clusters appear in mid summer, turning into cascades of brilliant blue berries by autumn. These legendary berries of jams, jellies, and wines are quite tasty though tart. Leaves are compound deciduous and leaflets elliptic with sharply toothed margins.

California Indians gathered not only the berries as snacks but the pithy branches were hollowed and used as whistles and clapper sticks in dances and ceremonies. The root was boiled and used as a healing lotion on cuts and scrapes.

Blue Elderberry

In the garden, this shrub grows in sun or part shade and is drought tolerant. Blue Elderberry takes pruning and is loved by wildlife.

Mar–Sep ● Ma, So, Na, Me
2–8 m, 7–25 ft

Red Elderberry
Sambucus racemosa
Honeysuckle Family,
Caprifoliaceae

The creamy white clusters of flowers of this native shrub have five small lobed petals. Leaves are compound with leaflets lance to egg shaped. Red Elderberry grows in moist open spaces near the coast and likes coastal fog. Berries of this elderberry are red and unlike its blue relative this fruit is **poisonous**. There is a great deal of variation in the species, so be extra cautious.

This shrub can be grown in sun or part shade. The berries attract birds.

Mar–Jul ● Ma, So, Na, Me
2–6 m, 7–20 ft

Red Elderberry

Snowberry
Symphoricarpos albus var. *laevigatus*
Honeysuckle Family, *Caprifoliaceae*

The small snow white berries of this native stream side shrub appear in late summer as the white to pinkish little bell shaped flowers of fade. The bush, with oval, dark green leaves, is also found in shady spots in the coastal forests and mixed woodlands.

A similar species is Creeping Snowberry, which as the name implies is a very low grower.

Snowberry can be grown in sun or part shade. Its berries attract birds.

May–Jul ● Ma, So, Na, Me
.6–1.8 m, 2–6 ft

Snowberry

Creeping Snowberry
Symphoricarpos mollis
Honeysuckle Family, *Caprifoliaceae*

Unlike its upright common cousin, native Creeping Snowberry is found spreading low close to the ground in canyons and forest openings. The white berries are in clusters and its name *mollis*, meaning soft in Latin, refers to the hairy, egg shaped leaves. The five lobed, pink petals form the bell shaped flowers.

Excellent low growing, deciduous shrub for the garden.

Apr–Jun ● Ma, So, Na, Me
1.5–6 m, 5–20 ft

Creeping Snowberry

Mountain Dogwood
Cornus nuttallii
Dogwood Family, *Cornaceae*

What more beautiful sign of spring can be found than the beautiful shrub and flower, the Mountain Dogwood. Thomas Nuttall (1786-1859), for whom this lovely deciduous shrub is named, was an eccentric exploring botanist of the west. This plant is a wonderful example of the representation of nature's wild beauty, growing to a height of 15 m, 50 ft. In bloom, they are magnificent. There are 4-7 white petals with large bracts, and the deciduous leaf is a broad elliptical shape. You will find this moisture loving, showy specimen in open to dense forest, usually in the mountains.

Apr–Jul ● Ma, So, Na, Me
2.4–15 m, 8–50 ft

Mountain Dogwood

Common Manzanita
Arctostaphylos manzanita
Heath Family, *Ericaceae*

Decorating the grasslands and chaparral are clumps of manzanita bushes. Their small grayish green, elliptical leaves are accented by peeling ocher red bark. Manzanita, meaning little apple in Spanish, is named for the smooth, little round, red berries of early summer. In spring, tiny, bell shaped, white to pink flowers decorate the bushes.

For California Indians this plant was a revered and useful shrub. The bark was boiled for tea to check diarrhea. The berries were dried and ground to be used in Pinole mixtures or mixed with water for a tasty paste spread. The hard wood was used in making many tools. The bright light from the burning wood was used at dances and other ceremonies.

A useful specimen and drought resistant shrub with beautiful form and bark.

Feb–Apr ● Ma, So, Na, Me
to 7 m, 23 ft

Common Manzanita

Salal

Gaultheria shallon
Heath Family, *Ericaceae*

This common evergreen shrub grows to 2 m, 6 ft, high in mixed coastal forests and openings in the Redwoods. The tiny urn shaped flowers are in small clusters among the alternate, simple, evergreen leaves.

The dark purple, rough skinned, rounded berries were eaten by California Indians.

Salal is a good large scale ground cover, particularly for under Redwoods where nothing else will grow. An excellent evergreen shrub that prefers moisture and more acid soil, but can tolerate less.

Apr–Jul ● Ma, So, Na, Me
.3–2 m, 1–6 ft

Salal

Western Labrador Tea

Ledum glandulosum
Heath Family, *Ericaceae*

Delicate white clusters of tiny five petaled flowers bloom on this stiff, shrubby plant. Leaves are alternate, simple, leathery, and evergreen, and the margins may be rolled under. Found in wet boggy places like its cousin, Western Azalea. The leaves have a scent between turpentine and strawberries.

The plant was used as a tonic and to treat colds, headaches, and arthritis by California Indians. Native Americans used the leaves to prepare a tea like beverage. It becomes toxic if cooked for a long time in a closed container.

Apr–Jul ● Ma, So, Me
.6–2 m, 2–7 ft

Western Labrador Tea

Pacific Rhododendron
Rhododendron macrophyllum
Heath Family, *Ericaceae*

The large, rosy pink, showy flower clusters of this native shrub are a welcoming sign of spring. The tall bushes with evergreen, elliptical, alternate leaves are found in highly acidic, nutrient poor, seasonally wet, sandy soils, often with a thick surface duff of acidic conifer litter beneath the towering coastal trees. As with any flowering shrub in the forest, they are a joy to come upon in bloom.

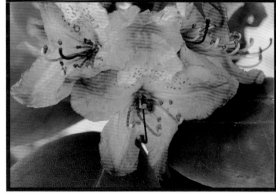

The flowers were used for wreaths in dances by California Indians.

A very attractive shrub with beautiful flowers to use as a specimen. Pacific Rhododendron needs highly acid soil.

Pacific Rhododendron

Apr–Jul ● Ma, So, Na, Me
1–5 m, 4–15 ft

Western Azalea
Rhododendron occidentale
Heath Family, *Ericaceae*

This delicate white bloom tinged with pink and orange is as lovely to behold as its fragrance is to experience. One may smell these flowers before they see them. The shrubs with their deciduous, alternate, simple, elliptic leaves are found along coastal streams, in moist openings amongst the trees, and wet meadows.

Foliage is toxic to livestock.

An attractive ornamental for moist, shady spots with beautiful flowers in spring.

Apr–Aug ● Ma, So, Na, Me
1–5 m, 4–15 ft

Western Azalea

Western Redbud
Cercis occidentalis
Pea Family, *Fabaceae*

Fluttering delicately in the breezes of coastal canyons, the rounded, heart shaped, smooth, glossy leaves of this little tree evoke serenity and grace. The lovely magenta pea shaped blooms, growing along the stems, appear from March through May. It is always a surprise to find this brilliantly colored gift of nature in the wild.

California Indians peeled young branches to be used in baskets and bark strips were woven into design elements.

A great plant for the first sign of spring. Long lived, pretty all year. Can be pruned as a single trunk or left as a multi trunk small tree. Should be underplanted with ground cover.

Mar–May ● Ma, So, Na, Me
2–6 m, 6–18 ft

Western Redbud

Spanish Broom
Spartium junceum
Pea Family, *Fabaceae*

A "dirty" word among wildflower enthusiasts, this invasive, nasty weed shows its yellow pea like flowers in almost any disturbed area. Obnoxious colonies of the spreading shrub can be seen overrunning whole hillsides which were once covered with native vegetation. The nearly leafless stems and the yellow blooms are easily recognized and should be eliminated in the wild. Cal-IPC rates it A in impact and B in invasiveness. Check Resources for more information.

Other similar alien invasive weeds are French Broom, Scotch Broom, and Gorse.

Apr–Jun ● Ma, So, Me
to 3 m, 10 ft

Spanish Broom

Yellow Bush Lupine

Lupinus arboreus
Pea Family, *Fabaceae*

The yellow lupine flowers of this shrubby bluff top dweller have the usual pea shape. Leaves are narrow and palm shaped. A very common shrub in sandy places. There is debate whether Yellow Bush Lupine is considered a native from Sonoma County south, and non native to the north where it was introduced.

California Indians used root fibers from this plant to make string for nets used in hunting and fishing.

A rapid grower in the garden, so consider it for a background plant. This beautiful shrub with long, yellow flower stalks is good on slopes. Toxic to sheep.

Mar–Jun ● Ma, So, Na, Me
1–2 m, 3–6 ft

Chaparral Pea
Pickeringia montana
Pea Family, *Fabaceae*

This spiny evergreen shrub has displays of beautiful rose magenta flowers. The petals are pea shaped with the leaf being compound with three leaflets, alternate, and evergreen. Leaflets are egg shaped with the leaf tips pointed. Twigs are stiff and spiny. The shrubs will sometimes form dense impenetrable thickets on dry hillsides and chaparral. Though the species name may be fun to roll off the tongue, the prickly plant is no fun to struggle through on a hike.

May–Aug ● Ma, So, Na, Me
1.8–2.1 m, 6–7 ft

Chaparral Pea

Golden Chinquapin
Chrysolepis chrysophylla
Oak Family, *Fagaceae*

This native evergreen shrub, sometimes tree, favors forests and woodlands. The leaves are alternate, simple, and generally taper at both ends. They are dark green above, golden brown below. Twigs have small golden colored scales. In summer, the strong odor of a profusion of flowers is sure to capture your attention. White male and female flowers in erect spreading clusters dominate the foliage. The fruit of their union is a spiny bur holding 1-3 nuts.

Trees live to be 400 or 500 years old. The largest lives in Mendocino County and is 37 m, 122 ft, tall.

This large, slow growing, evergreen shrub likes some moisture in the garden.

Jun–Sep ● Ma, So, Na, Me
Tree: 15–36 m, 50–120 ft
Shrub: to 4.5 m, 15 ft

Golden Chinquapin

Alkali Heath

Frankenia salina
Frankenia Family, *Frankeniaceae*

This salt excreting sub shrub of coastal salt marshes is common locally. Generally low to medium height, with twigs and leaves ranging from smooth to densely hairy. Leaves are entire, with margins rolled under. They are lightly

dusted with salt. Up close the leaves look thick and a bit fleshy. Flowers are white to dark pink or purple in attractive contrast to the dusky foliage. The petals form a long floral tube, then spread wide at the top. This sub shrub forms mats to 3 m, 10 ft, in diameter.

June–Oct ● Ma, So, Na
10–60 cm, 4–24 in

Alkali Heath

Coast Silk Tassel

Garrya elliptica
Silk-tassel Family, *Garryaceae*

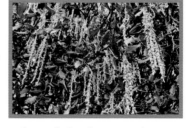

From winter to early spring, the silky tassels of this evergreen shrub may remind one of icicles, but without the freezing temperatures. The tassels are the yellowish male flower catkins that can grow to 25 cm, 10 in, long. This v shaped shrub to tree favors shady woodlands near the coast. The leaves are opposite, simple, leathery ovals. They are glossy dark green above and woolly gray below with the leaf margins turned under and undulating. On separate plants, shorter female tassels produce grape like, red purple berries.

A similar species, Fremont Silk Tassel, *Garrya fremontii*, is more likely to be found inland. Leaf margins are not wavy.

This is a good foundation shrub for the garden.

Jan–Mar ● Ma, So, Na, Me
8 m, 25 ft

Coast Silk Tassel

Hillside Gooseberry

Ribes californicum
Gooseberry Family, *Grossulariaceae*

Native to forest openings in the coastal ranges, this early blooming, deciduous shrub has greenish white, pendant flowers that are mighty magnets to hummingbirds and butterflies. Petals form small clusters of 1-3 tubular flowers with green to red sepals curved backward from the petals. Stamens jut out from the floral tube. The leaves are thin with round teeth, and if growing in full sun, will turn red in summer.

This is a good barrier plant for the garden. But do not plant it near walkways as the spiky stems are thorny. This plant is good for habitat gardens.

Feb–Mar ● Ma, So, Na, Me
to 1 m, 3 ft

Hillside Gooseberry

Pink-flowering Currant

Ribes sanguineum var. *glutinosum*
Gooseberry Family, *Grossulariaceae*

These cheerful pink flowers against their dark green foliage brighten many habitats in early spring, as this native shrub is widely spread across our region. Clusters of 10-15 pink to white, small tubular flowers are borne on droopy stems. Sepals and petals are both pink to white. Leaves are firm with shallow lobes. The upper surface is dark green with scattered hairs.

This native shrub is similar to Red-flowering Currant. But the flowers here are pink not crimson, the flower clusters droop and leaves are a little less hairy.

For the garden, this shrub makes good hedges.

Mar–Apr ● Ma, So, Na, Me
4 m, 12 ft

Pink-flowering Currant

Pitcher Sage
Lepechinia calycina
Mint Family, *Lamiaceae*

This large, wonderfully fragrant, lime green shrub with exceptional white to lavender flowers is a handsome member of the Mint Family. The leaves are large and lance like with square stems on a woody base. Mature leaves are dark green with lime green leaves at the growing tips. Five petals form a two lipped floral tube; the lower lip juts out while the upper lip reflexes. Numerous single blossoms emerge along the stems. Pitcher Sage is found on open slopes.

In the garden, Pitcher Sage likes sun and minimal water. It takes well to pruning.

Apr–Jun ● Ma, Me, Na, So
to 2 m, 7 ft

Pitcher Sage

Sonoma Sage

Salvia sonomensis
Mint Family, *Lamiaceae*

This low creeping perennial favors wind swept slopes where its fragrance may waft around you. The contrast of blue violet flowers above gray green leaves equally appeals to the senses. The petals form a two lipped floral tube, although the upper lip is nearly absent. Leaves are lance like to egg shaped, with a wonderful fragrance with or without gentle crushing.

Great low growing shrub with fragrant foliage and pretty flowers in spring. It is perfect for slope control or ground cover. Likes full sun and minimal water.

May–Jun ● Me, Na, So
10–40 cm, 4–16 in

Sonoma Sage

Bush Poppy

Dendromecon rigida
Poppy Family, *Papaveraceae*

The yellow flowers of this shrub are a welcome sight on dry slopes, stony washes, and recent burns. Fast growing in sun and fast draining soil, it is native to our area. The attractive poppy like

flowers of four bright yellow petals are 2-5 cm, 1-2 in, across growing at the ends of branches. The leaves are gray green, evergreen, very finely serrated, and lance shaped.

Use in the garden in dry sunny locations where a tough, long flowering evergreen is needed. It can grow quite tall.

Apr–Aug ● Ma, So, Na, Me
1–3 m, 3–10 ft

Bush Poppy ●

Buckbrush

Ceanothus cuneatus
Buckthorn Family, *Rhamnaceae*

This striking evergreen shrub is commonly found in chaparral. The small white, blue, or lavender flowers have five sepals and five concave petals, each of which envelops a stamen. Individual flowers are arranged in open, showy

clusters with flower stems the same color as the flowers. They have a heavy scent in full bloom. The small, dark green leaves are wedge to egg shaped, and typically clustered on short lateral branches.

A prized garden shrub for its striking display and spring long fragrance. This plant is drought resistant.

Mar–May ● Ma, So, Na, Me
to 3 m, 10 ft

Buckbrush

Wavyleaf Ceanothus
Ceanothus foliosus var. *foliosus*
Buckthorn Family, *Rhamnaceae*

An evergreen shrub that grows fairly commonly in rocky serpentine soils on dry slopes and ridges. It has small, dark green, elliptical leaves. The flowers are pale to deep dark blue, have five tiny petals and are pleasantly fragrant.

Native Americans used the plant to make baskets and for medicinal purposes.

This is a pretty ornamental plant for the garden. It prefers sun to light shade.

**Mar–May ● Ma, So, Na, Me
to 1 m, 3 ft**

Wavyleaf Ceanothus

Deer Brush
Ceanothus integerrimus
Buckthorn Family, *Rhamnaceae*

A loosely branched, woody shrub found in chaparral on mountain slopes. Leaves are thin, glossy, elliptical, and deciduous. They are somewhat hairy, dark green above, and lighter green below. Small white, deep to pale blue, or pink flowers with five tiny petals grow in clusters, less than 15 cm, 6 in, long at the end of branches. Twigs are slender, bright green, and often striped.

Native Americans used this plant medicinally and to make baskets.

In the garden, this plant is water tolerant and needs sun to light shade. Deer Brush is most valuable as a browse plant for wildlife.

**May–Jun ● So, Na, Me
to 4 m, 12 ft**

Deer Brush

Musk Brush

Ceanothus jepsonii var. *jepsonii*
Buckthorn Family, *Rhamnaceae*

A moderately low, sprawling, evergreen shrub commonly found on dry serpentine slopes, in chaparral, in full or partial sun. It has holly like elliptical leaves with 8-10 coarse spiny teeth and lavender to blue to white flowers. Flowers emerge in early spring. They have five tiny petals, grow in clusters, and produce a musky fragrance.

The flowers were used as soap by California Indians.

Mar–Apr ● Ma, So, Na, Me
to 1 m, 3 ft

Musk Brush

Toyon

Heteromeles arbutifolia
Rose Family, *Rosaceae*

This delightful holly like shrub is a favorite plant for holiday decorating and an abundant winter food source for birds, squirrels, and other wildlife. Also known as Christmas Berry, it is common to semi dry, brushy slopes and canyons. In late spring and early summer, showy, flat topped clusters of small white, five petaled flowers appear. By fall, clusters of slowly ripening berries emerge and turn brilliant red in winter. The long, elliptical, evergreen leaves are shiny dark green above, yellow green beneath, sharply serrated and leathery.

Native Americans ate the berries and made tea from the bark to soothe aches and pains.

This is a lovely shrub or hedge plant in sunny, dry spots in the garden.

Jun–Jul ● Ma, So, Na, Me
to 5 m, 16 ft

Toyon

Chamise

Adenostoma fasciculatum
Rose Family, *Rosaceae*

This medium to large evergreen shrub is a major component of chaparral. It is common on dry ridges and slopes, holds the soil against erosion, and protects the soil after fires. The shiny leaves are small and needle like and sprout in clusters from dry looking, stick like branches. Clusters of small white flowers with five petals and long stamens grow near the end of the branches.

Native Americans used the plant to make arrow points and the leaves for medicinal purposes.

This plant makes an excellent wind break or screen in the garden in full sun, with good drainage. It protects the soil after fire, as it re-sprouts from the base.

May–Jun ● Ma, So, Na, Me
to 4 m, 12 ft

Cream Bush
Holodiscus discolor
Rose Family, *Rosaceae*

This deciduous shrub displays cream colored sprays that look like ocean foam. It is found growing on cliffs overlooking the ocean and on north slopes in forests and woodlands. The five petaled flowers grow in showy white clusters from 10-25 cm, 4-10 in, in length. The leaves are alternate, deciduous, dull green, hairy, egg shaped with a broad to flat base, and toothed. This plant has a noticeably sweet scent that from a distance is very agreeable.

Native Americans used the straight branches to make arrow shafts and the bark and dried leaves as an antiseptic for cuts and abrasions.

In the garden, this plant favors partial shade and a little summer water.

Cream Bush

May–Aug ● Ma, So, Na, Me
1–6 m, 3–20 ft

Oso Berry
Oemleria cerasiformis
Rose Family, *Rosaceae*

This shrub is one of the first to leaf out in the spring. Common to canyons, brush land, and moist wooded ravines, it is wonderfully fragrant. The white, inconspicuous flowers grow in droopy clusters and are either male or female, with seed and pollen bearing flowers on separate plants. Leaves are oblong, deciduous, light green with smooth margins. Fruit is green to yellow to red, and black when mature.

Favoring sun and good water, this plant attracts birds and butterflies to the home garden.

Feb–Apr ● Ma, So, Na, Me
1–3 m, 3–10 ft

Oso Berry

California Wild Rose
Rosa californica
Rose Family, *Rosaceae*

This beautiful member of the Rose Family is commonly found in rather moist places where it forms thorny thickets. This Wild Rose is fragrant with five pink petals and many stamens. The leaves are deciduous and compound, with 5-7 elliptical leaflets. Stout prickles are straight or curved. This is the most common, abundant, and variable of the native roses.

Native Americans made tea from the bright red rose hip for medicinal purposes.

Recommended for the back of the garden where this California Wild Rose likes light shade and prefers some moisture.

**May–Aug ● Ma, So, Na, Me
to 3 m, 10 ft**

California Wild Rose

Wood Rose
Rosa gymnocarpa
Rose Family, *Rosaceae*

Commonly found in shady woods, this slender shrub member of the Rose Family has pink, five petaled flowers with many stamens. The deciduous leaves are elliptical and compound. The fruit becomes a hip. Prickles are straight and slender.

Native Americans made tea from the rose hip for medicinal purpose.

The Wood Rose prefers a shady spot in the garden. It is smaller and less invasive than the California Wild Rose.

**May–Jul ● Ma, So, Na, Me
to 1 m, 3 ft**

Wood Rose

Nootka Rose

Rosa nutkana var. *nutkana*
Rose Family, *Rosaceae*

Pale pink, five petaled flowers with many stamens grace this somewhat thorny shrub. Leaves are deciduous, compound and of an elliptical shape. Prickles are straight. Although uncommon, you can find this plant in damp woods, open slopes and flat places. As the name implies, Nootka Rose grows from Alaska south along the coast to our area.

As with other roses, a hip is formed which may be made into a tea.

May–Jul ● So, Me
to 2 m, 6 ft

Nootka Rose

Salmon Berry

Rubus spectabilis
Rose Family, *Rosaceae*

Occasionally found in thickets in moist areas, this tall shrub has clusters of 1-4 pinkish red flowers, each with five petals and many stamens. The maple like leaves are deciduous. The fruits are blackberry like. Its presence indicates that the soil is moist wherever it is growing.

The vegetation is mildly astringent and is sometimes used for medicinal purposes.

In the garden Salmon Berry likes shade and water.

Mar–Jun ● Ma, So, Me
to 3.5 m, 12 ft

Salmon Berry

Sticky Monkey Flower

Mimulus aurantiacus
Broom-rape Family, *Orobanchaceae*

Found commonly on rocky slopes throughout the rocky areas of much of California. Rich in nectar, this long blooming shrub provides an excellent food source for hummingbirds. The five petaled flowers united into the two lipped tube typical of *Mimulus*, are usually yellow orange to deep orange in color, but can also be white, yellow or red. The woody stems of this plant are covered with sticky secretions which give the plant its descriptive common name.

Juice of the plant can be used to soothe minor burns.

In the garden, Sticky Monkey Flower favors dry soil and lots of sun. A good shrubby perennial that, with moderate water, will be less stressed looking.

Recently moved from the Figwort Family, *Scrophulariaceae*.

Mar–Aug ● Ma, So, Na, Me
10–150 cm, 4–60 in

Sticky Monkey Flower

California Fremontia

Fremontodendron californicum
Cacao Family, *Sterculiaceae*

This large, branched, evergreen shrub is not often found locally. But taking the time to search for this lovely yellow treasure is definitely worth a hike along brushy slopes and chaparral. The petals of this showy flower are absent, but the petal like sepals in yellow, sometimes tinged with orange or red, are vividly set off by the hairy, evergreen foliage which itself is interesting with or without the flowers. Leaves are alternate, simple, leathery, and round to egg shaped. Margins are three lobed with tips round to pointed.

This very drought tolerant shrub with its short lived but showy flowers is used in gardens as a specimen plant. It really does not want any water for it to be successful. But be careful, touching the hairy leaves and stems may cause contact dermatitis.

May ● Ma, So, Na, Me
3–8 m, 10–25 ft

California Fremontia ●

Bigleaf Maple

Acer macrophyllum
Maple Family, *Aceraceae*

This lovely broadleaf, deciduous tree can be identified easily in the fall. Its leaves turn a greenish yellow, then bright lemon yellow, and then brown before they fall to the ground in the tree's stream side habitat. Yellowish green flowers form elongated clusters. With leaves palm shaped, opposite, and deciduous. Leaf size varies, but can be as large as 35 cm, 14 in. The seeds are winged samaras covered with stiff hairs.

Bigleaf Maple

Native California Indians used tea from ground bark for reducing fever and bark strips were used in basketry.

Bigleaf Maple is fast growing and delivers autumn colors and lovely flower catkin displays in spring. It can be drought tolerant in cooler, moist micro-climates, but will need regular water in hot dry areas.

Mar–Apr ● Ma, So, Na, Me
5–30 m, 15–100 ft

Red Alder

Alnus rubra
Birch Family, *Betulaceae*

This picturesque tree of coastal streams displays lovely drooping catkins which turn green in the spring. Then in fall, catkins become little brown empty cones after releasing their seed. The green, serrated edged leaves and the smooth gray mottled bark of this majestic tree are a pleas-

ant sight. This native's leaves are deciduous, alternate, simple with an elliptical shape, and the margins are tightly rolled under. Upper surfaces of the leaf are dark green and hairless with the under surface pale green with rust colored veins. This beautiful Birch is a favorite of many who may stop to rest by a clear, gently flowing, coastal creek.

Native Americans used the wood to smoke salmon and for medicinal purposes.

A similar tree is White Alder, *A. rhombifolia*, usually found further inland.

Mar–Apr ● Ma, So, Me
to 24 m, 80 ft

Red Alder

Pacific Madrone

Arbutus menziesii
Heath Family, *Ericaceae*

These stately members of the coastal woodland and chaparral communities have twisted reddish trunks, are widely branched with a full crown of oblong, smooth, dark green, evergreen leaves. Bark exfoliates revealing smooth, red brown inner bark. White to pink urn shaped petals are in clusters. Orange red berries adorn the tree in winter and is a good food source for birds. Flocks of Band-tailed Pigeons may be seen enjoying the fruit.

Rightfully so, Pacific Madrone is considered the most beautiful California native tree. A slow grower and best chances of survival are when planted from a small size container. Likes it roots in the shade and leaves in the sun. Worth the effort.

Pacific Madrone

Mar–May ● Ma, So, Na, Me
to 40 m, 140 ft

Black Oak

Quercus kelloggii
Oak Family, *Fagaceae*

Named for Albert Kellogg, California gold rush naturalist, a San Francisco physician, as well as founder of the California Academy of Sciences, this graceful crowned, dark barked, deciduous tree can be found in open woodlands. Lustrous green leaves are up to 20 cm, 8 in, long and deeply lobed with tiny spiked tips. Trees can live to be 500 years old. Black Oak hybridizes with Coast Live Oak.

The oblong to egg shaped acorn was gathered and prepared by California Indians as a staple annual protein source. Dyes were made from its bark.

A large, deciduous, drought tolerant tree with beautiful new growth and catkins in spring.

Mar–Apr ● Ma, So, Na, Me
to 20 m, 60 ft

Black Oak in spring

Canyon Live Oak

Quercus chrysolepis
Oak Family, *Fagaceae*

Canyon Live Oak has some similar characteristics to its coastal cousin, Coast Live Oak, *Q. agrifolia*, particularly the spiny oblong leaves. They are green above, smooth and bluish white below, and are quite thick and leathery. Leaves that are entire and others with spiny toothed margins may be found on the same tree. The tree's elongated acorn with a shallow, scaly cap, is 3-4

cm, 1-1¹/₂ in, long. Bark is thick, smooth to slightly furrowed, and grayish brown. Canyon Live Oak is found in woodlands and chaparral.

California Indians leached tannins from the acorns, making an edible mush.

This oak an excellent small specimen tree with some shade and moderate water.

Apr–May ● Ma, So, Na, Me
4.5–21 m, 15–70 ft

Canyon Live Oak

California Buckeye

Aesculus californica
Buckeye Family, *Hippocastanaceae*

In spring this small tree is quite appealing with its showy, white, fragrant flower spikes contrasted by broad veined, green leaves. Five petals form the showy clusters of scented flowers. In midsummer this plant is deciduous, dropping its leaves. In late summer large, dangling, flattened pear shaped fruits are on the tree. It favors growing in partial shade to full sun on dry slopes and canyons. All parts of the tree are **toxic**.

Used as an ornamental due to its year long interest and picturesque form.

May–Jun ●
Ma, So, Na, Me
1–3 m, 4–10 ft

California Buckeye, fresh spring leaves

Oak woodland in spring

Oak

Quercus spp.
Oak Family, *Fagaceae*

There is no genus of tree which typifies the variety of California habitats as does *Quercus*. These adept survivors have hybridized in the wild to thrive in dendrological diversity. With smooth to deeply furrowed bark, to small and spiny or large deeply lobed leaves, they represent variety. Leaves may be deciduous or evergreen. Small pollen bearing flowers are clustered in droopy catkins. They are usually found growing in woodlands and chaparrals. Their distinctively different forms are a pleasure to behold.

The different acorn fruits of these trees provided an ample available protein source for many California Indian groups.

A multitude of seasonal events and life forms occur in and around Oak trees. Animals and insects live in and on the tree. Microscopic fungi are also a part of the Oak's existence.

● **Ma, So, Na, Me**
Various heights

Oaks in fall color mixed with conifers

California Bay
Umbellularia californica
Laurel Family, *Lauraceae*

A large, wonderfully fragrant broad leaved evergreen tree found in woods, valleys, and forests. In the open it has a natural dome shaped crown. The leaves are oblong, lustrous, and aromatic; dark green and shiny above, paler and smooth below. When crushed they are highly aromatic but may irritate the eyes and nose. The flowers are inconspicuous, small and yellow to green to red. Also known as Oregon Myrtle and Bay Laurel.

The leaves are used in cooking but are much more potent than commercial bay leaf.

Native Americans used it as an insect repellent and to treat headaches and rheumatism.

This tree with its wonderfully fragrant foliage is a favorite for large scale landscaping, parks, and specimen gardens.

Dec–May ● Ma, So, Na, Me
9–24 m, 30–80 ft

California Bay ●

Oregon Ash
Fraxinus latifolia
Olive Family, *Oleaceae*

This tree is fast growing for the first third of its long life, then grows slowly afterward. It is common in canyons and along the banks of streams. Flowers are insignificant, have no petals and both male and female are on the same plant. Leaves are deciduous, compound, formed of 5-7 leaflets. In late summer, clusters of greenish winged samaras are very prominent. Seeds are wind dispersed in early fall. The seeds are eaten by birds and squirrels. Oregon Ash can live to be 250 years old.

In Oregon, Native Americans believed that poisonous snakes avoided stands of this tree.

This tree is good in lawns with beautiful yellow gold autumn color.

Mar–May ● Ma, So, Na, Me
9–22 m, 30–75 ft

Oregon Ash

Douglas-fir

Pseudotsuga menziesii
Douglas-fir Family, *Pinaceae*

Named for the intrepid Scot who, with his terrier Billy, walked the fields, forests and woodlands of coastal California in 1832. David Douglas' name is associated with many plant species but most appropriately with this, the most desirable building lumber in the world. His name and fame have spread with the use of this lumber, but perhaps he would have liked to see more of these co-nifers standing tall in their varied habitats than laying low at the mill. The distinc-tive 5-8 cm, 2-3 in, cone appears to have bracts that resemble the rear portions of mice with tails and legs protruding from the scales. The slightly spiny needles are spirally disposed along the rough barked twigs.

● Ma, Me, Na, So
to 68 m, 225 ft

Douglas-fir

Pacific Yew

Taxus brevifolia
Yew Family, *Taxaceae*

This small evergreen tree can reach 15 m, 50 ft, in height but it is usually much shorter. Single evergreen needles, about 3 cm, 1 in, long, are arranged in flat sprays on branching twigs. Each needle has a pointed, though not sharp tip. Pacific Yew is dioecious, with each plant being a separate sex, but occasional individuals can change sex with time. The female seed cones are highly modi-fied, each containing a single seed which develops into a bright red berry like

structure. The male cones are greenish. Both are borne on the lower sides of branches. This tree is slow growing, but can reach a ripe old age of 250-350 years old.

Apr–May ● Ma, So, Me
to 15 m, 50 ft

Pacific Yew, male cones ●

California Nutmeg

Torreya californica
Yew Family, *Taxaceae*

This dark evergreen tree is widely distributed in the shady canyons and along the mountain streams of central and northern California. The needles are flat, slightly curved with a pointed tip, and arranged in two rows of nearly opposite pairs. They are dark green above and light green with two pale lines below. The seed cone looks like a large olive and is very aromatic. It is green, sometimes striped with purple, and contains a very large seed.

Native Americans used the wood for bows, and the needles for tattooing.

Apr–May ● Ma, So, Na, Me

California Nutmeg ●

Coast Redwood

Sequoia sempervirens
Bald Cypress Family, *Taxodiaceae*

This beautiful red hued tree was named for the revered Cherokee scholar Sequoyah. Once blanketing the fog shrouded coastal zone from Oregon to Big Sur, California, with huge stands of 90 m, 300 ft, giants, less than one percent of its former range remains in old growth forest. The use of Redwood as lumber brought about its demise. The tiny one inch cones produce miniscule brown seeds which transform into the world's tallest trees. The dark green shiny leaves are on one plane on the twig, flat, and needlelike. No grander tree exists. Entering an old growth forest is like entering a centuries old cathedral.

Fast growing, Redwood likes water and sun to part sun. Goes well in a lawn or used to create a conifer shade garden.

● Ma, Me, Na, So
to 90 m, 300 ft

Coast Redwood ●

HOT SPOTS FOR WILDFLOWERS
Marin County

Marin Coastal
1. **China Camp State Park:** Coastal salt marsh, mixed evergreen forest. Gum Plant, California Cord-grass.
2. **Point Reyes National Seashore:** Douglas-fir forest, Bishop Pine forest, coastal grassland, freshwater marsh, salt marsh, beach and dunes, rocky headlands. Too many plants to mention! If it grows in northern California central coastal area, likely it can be found here. The marshes have Common Camas at its southern limit in May. The grassy headlands have fine blue Gentians in July.
3. **Marin Headlands:** Marsh and lagoon flora, open grasslands and northern coastal scrub communities. Special plants here include Matchweed, Franciscan Wallflower, Fragrant Everlasting.

Marin Inland
4. **Ring Mountain:** Serpentine grasslands and springs/seeps. Good place to see Mariposa Lilies and Star-tulips, Marin Western Flax, Tiburon Buckwheat, Tiburon Paintbrush.
5. **Muir Woods National Monument:** Coast Redwood forest. Understory plants include Western Coltsfoot, Leopard Lily, Western Trillium, and the uncommon *Montia diffusa* at its southern limit.
6. **Mt. Tamalpais State Park:** Serpentine grassland, chaparral shrubs of serpentinite and sandstone soils.
7. **Rock Spring:** Grassland plants such as Goldfields, Brewer's Locoweed, *Phacelia divaricata*, early Clarkia, Baby Blue Eyes. Higher up the mountain are *Ceanothus* and *Arctostaphylos*. The prettiest Manzanita is the winter-blooming, shell pink flowered Hoary Manzanita.
8. **Marin Municipal Water District Lands:** Grasslands, coast range mountain meadows, mixed evergreen forest, Lagunitas Meadows on the north side of Mt. Tamalpais has Serpentine Star Lily and Large Flower Star Tulip. The Carson ridge above Fairfax has serpentine chaparral and several rare associated plants such as Marin Navarretia and Marin Lessingia.
9. **Samuel P. Taylor State Park:** Mixed evergreen forest, Redwood forest, streamside vegetation including Smith's Fairy Bells, streamside Violets, Stream Orchid.
10. **Mt. Burdell Open Space Preserve:** Fine expanses of woodland, oak savannah and grassland, best for early wildflowers such as Owl's Clover, Star Lily.

Marin County
Location of Hot Spots on Public Lands

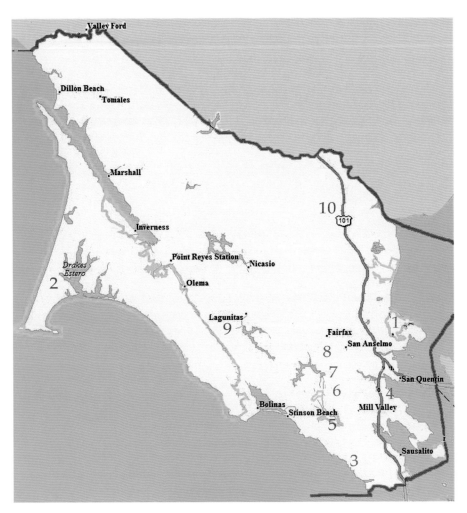

HOT SPOTS FOR WILDFLOWERS
Sonoma County

Sonoma Coastal

11. **Sonoma County State Beaches**: **Kortum Trail** from Goat Rock south. Coastal bluff and coastal prairie flowers of Iris, Paintbrush, and Lupine. Best late April to June. Gorgeous ocean views.
12. **Sonoma County State Beaches: Pinnacle Gulch Coastal Access** (near Bodega). Wildflower displays are long lasting with Lupine bushes, Salmonberry, Sticky Monkey Flowers, and California Poppies.
13. **Salt Point State Park:** Salt Point to Stump Beach - Coastal bluffs and prairie and in good years the headlands are carpeted with wildflowers such as Lupine, California Poppy, Seathrift, and Goldfields, May to July.
14. **Sea Ranch:** Various coastal bluff trails with access points and parking along Hwy. 1. Coastal bluffs and prairie wildflowers with Yellow Bush Lupine from May to July.
15. **Kruse Rhododendron State Reserve:** Rhododendron Loop and Chinese Gulch for beautiful close up views of wild Rhododendrons and Trillium.

Sonoma Inland

16. **Annadel State Park:** Steve's S Trail connecting to South Burma Trail. Trails climb through a forest of Douglas-fir with many ferns and Wood Rose. Continue to meadows of Blue-eyed Grass, Goldfields, and Lupine.
17. **Austin Creek State Recreation Area & Armstrong Redwoods:** Gilliam Creek Trail starts in woodlands of California Bay, Black Oak, and Maple. Early bloomers start in March. Climb through grassland and a steep climb to a serpentine swale.
18. **City of Sonoma, Overlook Trail:** Trailhead is just north of Veteran's Building and cemetery, about 2 blocks north of the plaza. Great spring wildflowers, views of downtown Sonoma and Mount Tamalpais to the south. Best late March to June.
19. **Foothill Regional Park:** Trails are wide, mostly rolling hills with some beautiful views and wildflower displays. February to May for Blue Dicks, Shooting Stars, Buttercups, and Butter and Eggs.
20. **Sonoma Valley Regional Park:** Good spring wildflowers along paved and unpaved trails. Gently rolling oak woodlands.
21. **Lake Sonoma:** Wolfow Trail off of Serpentine Trail in Liberty Glen Campground. Great diversity of wildflowers throughout the park, as well as native woodlands, including redwoods. Flowers include Indian Warrior, California Indian Pink, Blue-eyed Grass, various Iris, and Buttercups.
22. **Sugarloaf Ridge State Park:** Oak woodland and mixed evergreen forest. Grasslands on serpentine. One of the state's easternmost Coast Redwood forests occurs in the park.

Sonoma County
Location of Hot Spots on Public Lands

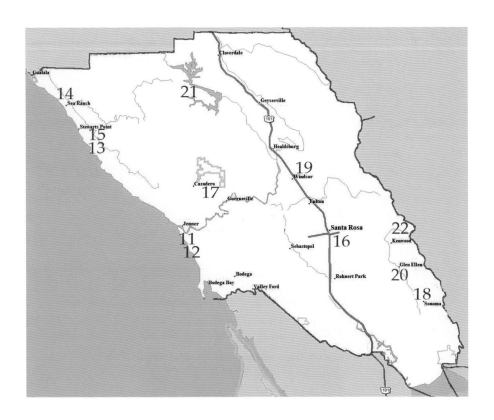

HOT SPOTS FOR WILDFLOWERS
Napa County

NAPA COUNTY

23. **Skyline Park:** In the hills east of Napa, off Imola Ave. Many trails and different habitats. Spring is best with sheets of Baby White Eyes, Shooting Stars, Lupines and Buttercups. Hound's Tongue, Zigadene and Trillium are found in shady areas.
24. **Bothe-Napa Valley State Park:** Calypso Orchid blooms here in early March. Trillium, Coltsfoot, Dutchman's Pipe and Fairy Bells are also found in the Redwood forest.
25. **Robert Louis Stevenson State Park:** Hike to the Palisades where volcanic and serpentine areas provide a diversity of plants. Difficult to strenuous hiking, but worth it for the flowers and views.
26. **Lake Hennessey:** The north end of the lake is accessible from Conn Valley Road. Lupines, several Clarkias, Delphiniums, Mule Ears and Golden Fairy Lantern can be found in the area.
26a. **Chiles/Pope/Snell Valleys:** Not a public area but a beautiful drive in the spring with a great diversity of wildflowers. The best displays are about a mile up Snell Valley. Remember, this is private property, so please do not trespass.

Napa County
Location of Hot Spots on Public Lands

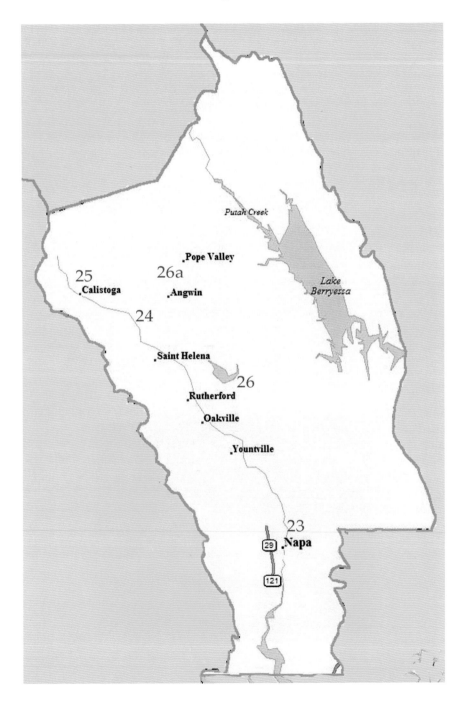

HOT SPOTS FOR WILDFLOWERS
Mendocino County

Mendocino Coastal

27. **Van Damme State Park:** The Fern Canyon Trail is a prime example of lush, older second-growth forest, with a vast array of perennials, ferns, liverworts and majestic conifers. The trail borders a creek where one can see large, leafy liverworts, and sometimes juvenile salmon.

28. **Eight Mile:** Not an official hiking area, but a beautiful drive with a wide variety of spring wildflowers.

29. **Headlands** for easy viewing of coastal wildflowers:
    a. West of the town of Mendocino
    b. MacKerricher State Park

Mendocino Inland

30. **Montgomery Woods State Reserve:** Various mosses and Redwood forest flowering community. Mixed conifer/oak woodlands and grassland habitat.

31. **Low Gap Park, Mendocino County Park:** Hillside and creek trails and is a very good close in area for mosses and wildflowers throughout the seasons.

32. **North Cow Mountain Recreation Area:** Mayacamas Trail along Willow Creek for many wildflower species through mid summer.

33. **Lake Mendocino** (U.S. Corps of Engineers): Good trails that pretty much surround the lake. Mixed Oak/Douglas-fir woodland with good wildflower variety throughout the season. Trails found on the south side of the dam are rich in flowers, ferns and mosses.

Mendocino County

Location of Hot Spots on Public Lands

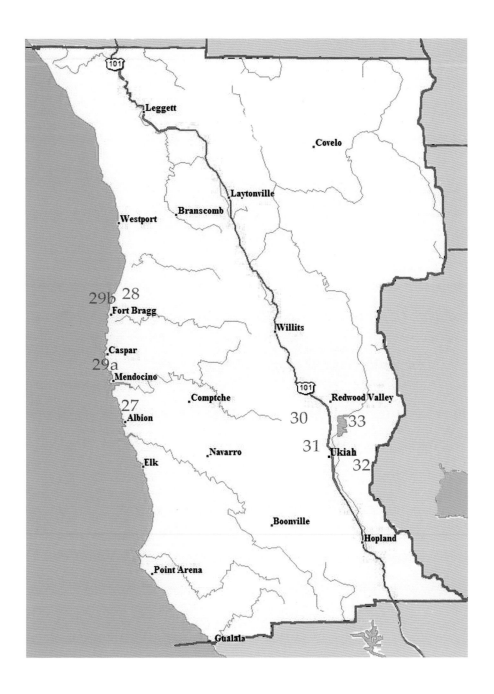

Leggett

Covelo

Laytonville

Branscomb

Westport

29b 28
Fort Bragg

Willits

Caspar

29a
Mendocino

Comptche

101

Redwood Valley

27
Albion

30

33

31

Navarro

Ukiah

Elk

32

Boonville

Hopland

Point Arena

Gualala

RESOURCES

ORGANIZATIONS

California Native Plant Society www.cnps.org (916) 447-2677

CNPS Marin Chapter www.marin.cc.ca.us/cnps

CNPS Milo Baker Chapter (Sonoma County) www.cnpsmb.org

CNPS Napa Valley Chapter (Napa County) www.ncfaa.com/skyline/cnps.html

CNPS Sanhedrin Chapter (inland Mendocino County) www.alt2is.com/cnps-sanhedrin

CNPS Dorothy King Young Chapter (coastal Mendocino County) www.dkycnps.org

Cal-IPC, California Invasive Plant Council www.cal-ipc.org (510) 843-3902

Marin/Sonoma Weed Management Areas www.marinsonomaweedmanagement.org

PCA Working Group www.nps.gov/plants/alien

The Nature Conservancy www.nature.org Search for "weeds"

Global Invasive Species Initiative tncweeds.ucdavis.edu

California Dept. of Fish & Game www.dfg.ca.gov Search for "rare plants"

PCI, Pacific Coast Iris www.pacificcoastiris.org (707) 964-3907

Pepperwood Preserve www.pepperwoodpreserve.org (707) 542-2080

The Bishop's Ranch www.bishopsranch.org (707) 433-2440

Fairfield Osborn Preserve www.sonoma.edu/org/preserve
(707) 664-3053

Marin Headlands www.nps.gov/archive/goga/mahe/

Marin Municipal Water District Lands www.marinwater.org

Check the web for hikes that may not be on public lands
sponsored by: CNPS, Sierra Club, Audubon Club, county Land
Trusts, The Nature Conservancy, Sonoma Ecology Center, and
more.

LOCAL NATIVE PLANT NURSERIES

Marin County
Larner Seeds, www.larnerseeds.com (415) 868-9407
Mostly Natives Nursery, www.mostlynatives.com (707) 878-2009

Sonoma County
California Flora Nursery, www.calfloranursery.com (707) 528-8813
North Coast Native Nursery, www.northcoastnativenursery.com
(707)769-1213

Napa County
Skyline Wilderness Park, Martha Walker Native Habitat Garden,
www.skylinepark.org (707)252-0481

Mendocino County
Anderson Valley Nursery, Boonville (707) 895-3853
The Calypso Orchid Company, Philo, calypsoorchid.com
Mendocino College Horticultural Dept., Ukiah -
Special plant sales and contract work and retail sales.
Red Tail Farms, Wholesale - 9000 Busch Lane, Potter Valley

Bay Area
Yerba Buena Nursery, www.yerbabuenanursery.com (650)851-1668
Annies Annuals, www.anniesannuals.com (510)215-1671

Northern California
Far West Bulb Farm, californianativebulbs.com

Local chapters of the California Native Plant Society have plant
sales during the year. See Organizations for web site addresses.

REFERENCES

Reference sources used in gathering information for this guide:

A California Flora, Munz

A Field Guide to Pacific States Wildflowers, Niehaus and Ripper

A Flora of Sonoma County, Best, Howell, Knight and Wells

Calflora, www.calfora.org

California Native Plants, www.californiagardens.com

Marin Flora, Howell

Plants of the Coast Redwood Region, Lyons and Cuneo-Lazaneo

Plants of the San Francisco Bay Region, Kozloff and Beidleman

Spring Wildflowers of the San Francisco Bay Region, Sharsmith

The Jepson Manual, Hickman

Treatment from the Jepson Manual, online at ucjeps.berkeley.edu

Trees and Shrubs of California, Stuart and Sawyer

Wildflowers of The Sea Ranch, Mahaffey

PHOTO & ILLUSTRATION CREDITS

All photographs are by the author except the following for which the individual artist retains all copyrights:

Peter Baye - Salt Rush, page 201

Bob Case - Periwinkle, page 180

Gerald & Buff Corsi/Focus on Nature, Inc. – Bush Poppy, page 224; California Fremontia, page 231; California Bay, page 236

Gary Hundt – image of Reny in the field, back cover

Mary Killian - Coyote Brush male flowers, page 211

Daniel F. Murley – Fringed Corn Lily, page 21; Douglas-fir, page 237, Coast Redwood, page 238

Doreen Smith – Woodland Strawberry, page 52; Philadelphia Fleabane, page 55; Footsteps of Spring, page 77; Charming Centaury, page 145; Pacific Yew, page 237

Vishnu – Corn Lily, page 24

Charles Younger – Broadleaf Arrowhead, page 18

Tenaya Gordon – Flower and leaf illustrations, pages 263-265; plant family icons throughout the guide and on the back cover

Keith Parker – Poetry throughout the guide

William Blake (1757-1827) – The Wild Flower's Song excerpt, page III

TECHNICAL NOTES ON PHOTOGRAPHY

For many years I have used a simple Nikon F camera with a handheld Pentax Spotmeter V. I have three lenses used for wildflowers: Micro-Nikkor 55 mm, Micro-Nikkor 60 mm, Nikkor 28 mm. Fuji Velvia is my choice of film for my Nikon F. For working on this guide, I started using a Nikon D50 digital camera. Since I took almost 8,000 images in 2006, it was good that I was using digital. The two Micro-Nikkor lenses work on the Nikon D50 as well. Because I use micro lenses, shoot up close, and generally use ASA 50 or 100, the depth of field in my images is very narrow. This accounts for their usually being one area of focus in the picture. All photography is done with natural lighting.

As wildflowers like to dance around in the wind, I use a white umbrella and/or special translucent plastic to help keep the plant from moving about and to provide light diffusion. Also, I use a Gitzo Explorer tripod unless I have my camera stabilized on the ground for low angle shots.

I respect wildflowers and appreciate their beauty. I do not pick wildflowers, and hope that you will not pick them either.

Index

FLOWER ARRANGEMENTS ON STEM

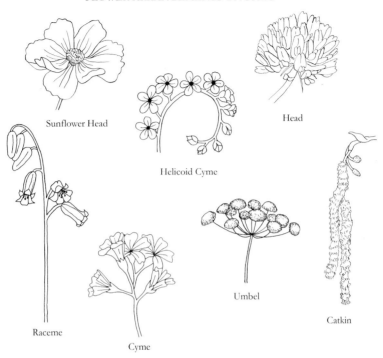

Sunflower Head

Head

Helicoid Cyme

Raceme

Cyme

Umbel

Catkin

FLOWER SYMMETRY

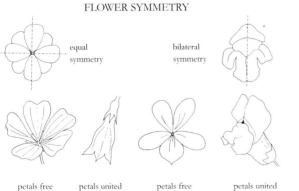

equal symmetry

bilateral symmetry

petals free   petals united   petals free   petals united

Regular shaped   Irregular shaped

GENERAL FLOWER PARTS

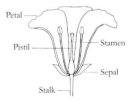

Petal

Pistil

Stamen

Sepal

Stalk

LEAF SHAPES

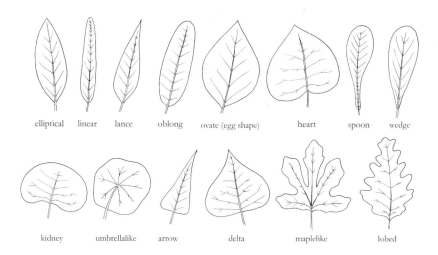

elliptical   linear   lance   oblong   ovate (egg shape)   heart   spoon   wedge

kidney   umbrellalike   arrow   delta   maplelike   lobed

LEAF ARRANGEMENTS

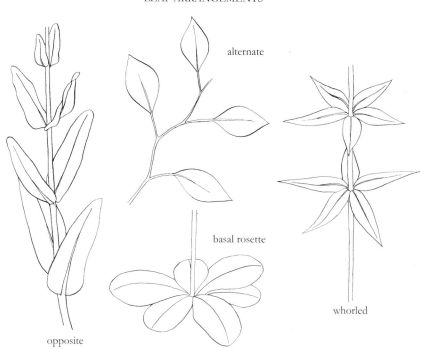

alternate

basal rosette

whorled

opposite

PARTS OF A LEAF

SIMPLE LEAF

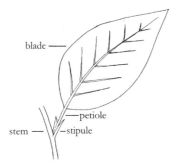

COMPOUND LEAVES

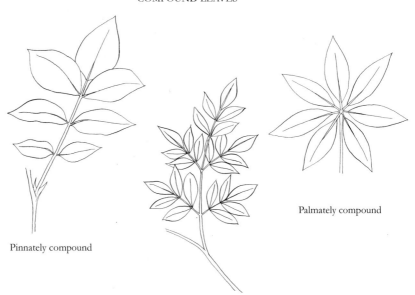

Pinnately compound

Palmately compound

Bipinnately compound